STANLEY GIBBONS STAMP COLLEC'

STAMP COLLECTING

HOW TO ARRANGE AND WRITE-UP A STAMP COLLECTION

STANLEY GIBBONS STAMP COLLECTING SERIES

STAMP COLLECTING

HOW TO ARRANGE AND WRITE-UP A STAMP COLLECTION

STANLEY PHILLIPS AND C. P. RANG
REVISED BY MICHAEL BRIGGS

STANLEY GIBBONS PUBLICATIONS LTD LONDON AND RINGWOOD

Published by Stanley Gibbons Publications Ltd
Editorial, Sales Offices and Distribution Centre:
Parkside, Christchurch Road, Ringwood,
Hants BH24 3SH

How to Arrange and Write-up a Stamp Collection was first published in 1933. The sixth edition was published as a *Stanley Gibbons Guide* in 1978. This seventh (revised) edition was published in 1983 and reprinted as a paperback in 1988.

First reprint 1990

Also in Stanley Gibbons Stamp Collecting Series:
Stamp Collecting – How to Start
Stamp Collecting – How to Identify Stamps
Stamp Collecting – Collecting by Theme
Stanley Gibbons Guide to Stamp Collecting
Stamp Collecting – Philatelic Terms Illustrated

Text pages designed by Julia Lilauwala; cover design by John Clark and Associates.
Printed in Great Britain by
BAS Printers Limited, Over Wallop, Hampshire

ISBN 0-85259-193-4
S.G. Item No. 2763

Contents

The Authors

Frederick Stanley Phillips was born in 1891, son of William H. Phillips and nephew of Charles J. Phillips who had purchased the entire stock, goodwill and trading name of Stanley Gibbons and Company the previous year. Stanley joined his uncle's company on leaving school in 1906 – initially employed on routine office work, including book-keeping, and later philatelic work. In 1910 he penned his first article for *Gibbons Stamp Weekly* – the first of many articles in a distinguished career in philatelic writing. After war service he returned to Gibbons to start the *Stanley Gibbons Monthly Circular*, renamed *Gibbons Stamp Monthly* in 1928 when Phillips became sole Editor. He had already been appointed Editor of the famous *Stanley Gibbons Stamp Catalogue* in 1922 and remained Editor until his death. In 1926 he became Joint Managing Director of Stanley Gibbons, sole Managing Director in 1946 and Chairman in 1953. Mr. Phillips died suddenly the following year – missing by two years the centenary of the firm he served for so long. As well as this book, he wrote several others including *Stamp Collecting* (also published in this series) and *The Splendid Book of Postage Stamps.*

Charles Peter Rang was born in 1901 and following a childhood in New Zealand and Australia and an education in France (University of Lyon) settled in England in 1919 joining the stamp company run by F. B. Smith. Rang joined Gibbons in 1924 and soon became involved in philatelic writing – contributing his first 'Through the Magnifying Glass' article to *Gibbons Stamp Monthly* in 1929. He worked closely with Stanley Phillips with whom he became joint Editor of the magazine in 1947 and sole Editor following Phillips' death in 1954 until his own untimely death in 1963. Apart from philately, he was keenly interested in boats and sailing, becoming an accomplished amateur boatbuilder.

The Reviser

Michael Briggs joined Stanley Gibbons in 1964, working initially in their famous 391 Strand shop, later specialising in display and exhibition work. In 1971 he transferred to the publishing side of the company working on *Gibbons Stamp Monthly* of which he is now News and Art Editor responsible for the 'Newsdesk' feature and the presentation of the magazine. A stamp collector for over 25 years, Mr. Briggs specialises in the stamps and postal stationery of Great Britain, the Channel Islands and the Isle of Man as well as maintaining collections of the stamps of Italy and Australia. He has a thematic interest – stamps and postmarks illustrating the history of London.

Introduction

It has been estimated that there are some two million stamp collectors in Great Britain, throughout the world there are many millions more. How many of these are hoarders – keeping their stamps in old envelopes or boxes – rather than intelligent collectors? It is not until stamps are arranged into an easily examined and logical order that they become a collection and cease to be an accumulation

The easiest way of achieving this is to house the stamps in some form of album. The beginner with many stamps from around the world will probably choose one of the many whole-world albums containing pages with printed headings for each stamp issuing country. Sooner or later, however, the increasing number of stamps being issued will force the collector to adopt some form of limitation – this may be a one-country or area collection, a specialised study, the collecting of stamps illustrating a particular theme or a postal history collection. Whatever the choice the use of some form of 'blank' loose-leaf album in which to arrange and describe the collection is almost certain.

This, however, calls for a certain measure of skill and judgement on the collector's part if a satisfactory result is to be achieved. Stamps must be arranged in a logical and pleasing manner and descriptions explaining the items shown have to be applied to the album pages. Such descriptions may repeat information found in a stamp catalogue or be the result of wider reading in general reference books, stamp magazines or specialised philatelic handbooks. The collector will, then, be required to apply many skills: mounting not only single stamps but also items such as blocks and covers in an attractive way; to select appropriate descriptive material that tells the story of the collection in a succinct style; to write or print it neatly to provide a well balanced and attractive album page.

Whatever kind of collection is formed it pays to treat it in the best possible manner. Often collections worth considerable sums are poorly housed and mounted, with no write-up or, at best, scrawled notes, and are stored in damaging conditions. A little time and effort spent on the treatment of items that may have been obtained at considerable expense is likely to pay dividends. Valuable and often fragile items will be less likely to suffer irreparable damage. Although a dealer will not pay for pretty writing-up, he is likely to be influenced by a neat and well-ordered collection – it will save time and expense in remounting and pricing and ensure that items are not overlooked when making a valuation. Of greater importance, perhaps, is the satisfaction that will be received from having formed a collection that may proudly be shown to friends – the result of the collector's own efforts.

It is hoped that this book will direct collectors, especially those who feel that they lack artistic inspiration, along the right lines, for not until they have learned to appreciate the advantages of proper mounting and writing-up will they gain maximum pleasure from the hobby of stamp collecting.

PART

1

Housing the collection

The first problem faced by the collector seems a straightforward one – which of the many loose-leaf albums to choose?

Those collecting just one or two countries may decide to house them in one of the many printed one-country albums available. These albums, with their printed spaces for stamps (often illustrated) and descriptions, present the collector with no problems of arrangement or writing-up; annual supplements allow the inclusion of new issues. For the 'simple-lifer', or those with a side-line collection, such an album will probably prove ideal; the keen collector will soon realise its limitations. Items will be acquired, such as blocks, varieties and covers, for which the printed album does not cater; it is also likely to contain spaces for scarce and expensive items that the collector is never likely to obtain, and which will remain for ever blank. It is then that the scope and freedom afforded by a 'blank' album becomes apparent. For those forming a specialised study or thematic collection such an album has been essential from the start.

Such albums fall into three main types: spring-back, ring-fitting and peg-fitting. Each type has advantages and disadvantages; only by examining and handling each can a collector choose for himself, but the following descriptions and illustrations will serve as a useful guide.

It is a false economy to buy a cheap album. After a comparatively short period of use a cheap album will begin to show signs of wear and the loose-leaf mechanism may cease to work properly. Buy the best album that funds will allow, bearing in mind that as your collection expands you will have to add to the series. A good album will give a lifetime's service if carefully handled and in general represents better value for money than a cheap one.

SPRING-BACK ALBUMS

The long established and popular spring-back album grips the leaves with vertical springs concealed in the binding. To release them the cover is opened out and folded back against the springs, the leaves are then slid out. The main disadvantage of the spring-back album is that the leaves will not lie flat when the album is open, though double linen-hinged leaves are available which lie flatter. Removing or adding even one page to the collection requires the removal of all leaves from the binder.

1 (*top left*) **Opening a spring-back album. Note how the cover has to be folded back against the springs**
2 (*top right*) **The binding mechanism of a multi-ring album. Levers at the bottom open it and those at the top close it**
3 (*below left*) **Removing the leaves from a peg-fitting album**
4 (*below right*) **Typical album pages: peg-fitting leaves with double linen-hinge and interleaving; transparent postcard, cover and booklet album pages**

RING-FITTING ALBUMS

Of increased popularity in recent years are the ring-fitting albums. These hold the leaves by a varying number of rings in the binding. The simplest kinds have three or four rings which are opened by pulling them apart. More complex are the albums with multi-rings – usually 22. These are opened and closed by means of levers at the top and bottom of the binding. Both types of binder hold the leaves fairly loosely, those with fewer rings more so than the multi-rings, they are thus more prone to damage. They have the advantage that the leaves lie flat wherever the album is opened, neither is it necessary to remove all the leaves when adding or removing a page from the binder.

PEG-FITTING ALBUMS

These albums have pegs, usually two, on to which the leaves are fitted, a locking mechanism inside the front cover secures the top of the pegs. As with spring-back albums the leaves do not always lie completely flat when the album is open, and some peg-fitting albums have double linen-hinged leaves which lie flatter.

LEAVES

The leaves of an album are even more important than the cover. There are two main types – those made in one piece and with the inside margin 'fluted' (ridged) to give flexibility at the side where the leaf is gripped by the binder and those which have a double linen-hinge. The latter have the advantage of lying flatter in albums with spring-back or peg fittings. Ring-binders, of course, do not require leaves that flex and leaves for these are neither fluted nor hinged.

There are nearly as many kinds of leaves as there are classes of paper and the collector who wishes to write-up a collection with pen and ink should pay great attention to this point when selecting an album. A good, hard, matt-surfaced cartridge paper is the most popular choice. Most leaves have a white or off-white finish and are generally to be preferred over black leaves. These were once quite popular and are still obtainable, they have, however, serious disadvantages. The most obvious is the difficulties that a black surface presents when writing-up, but another, no less important, problem is the danger that the colour of the leaf, especially in damp climates, may transfer itself to the stamps.

The leaves of most blank loose-leaf albums have *quadrillé* ruling upon them. These tiny squares are invaluable in working out how to position stamps on a page, as by counting them it is possible to lay out stamps symmetrically. The exact centre of the *quadrillé* area is normally indicated by a slight thickening of the ruling. The centre of the top, bottom and side margins of the mounting area is usually similarly marked. The *quadrillé* ruling is usually printed in a pale grey or yellow colour, it should be easily seen in order to guide the positioning of stamps but not be so prominent as to distract from them.

Peg-fitting albums and ring-fitting albums of the type with only a few rings have the disadvantage that with frequent use, and especially if the leaves have heavy items mounted on them, the holes punched in the page may eventually tear.

The best way to protect such pages is to use paper reinforcement rings, which are readily available from most stationers. These are circular pieces of white card, gummed on one side, with a hole cut out of the centre, and they very conveniently match the size of ring or peg most commonly used for stamp albums. The reinforcement rings are glued to the leaves so that their holes fit over the punched holes which fit the binder. Make sure that you do not use the self-adhesive type of reinforcement rings, the adhesive of which is liable, over some time, to seep from the edges of the ring, spoiling your leaves, album and possibly your stamps. Peg-fitting albums with double linen-hinged leaves are unlikely to require reinforcement as the linen hinge will give the leaf additional strength.

INTERLEAVING

Transparent interleaving is a very important part of a loose-leaf album. The best type is made of a thin glazed translucent paper. Clear plastic or acetate interleaves are best avoided; they can become charged with static, attracting dust and dirt and making them difficult to handle. Interleaving prevents stamps from rubbing against the back of the preceding page, and its use is advisable (especially in ring-fitting albums) in order to protect stamps from damage. With black leaves its use is essential. It can, of course, be dispensed with if a collection is mounted entirely in protective mounts.

Interleaving is available cut to size to fit most albums, and some leaves have it already attached, such leaves are far easier to handle. It should be noted however, that leaves with attached interleaving will not fit into a typewriter, and those collectors contemplating the use of this method of writing-up will have to use separate interleaves or attach them themselves to the album leaf after writing-up. This can be done by one or two dabs of a light paper glue in the left-hand margin of the leaf. Do not use adhesive tape, this adds to the bulk of the album and may seep after a few years.

SPECIAL ALBUMS

Many philatelic items, such as first day covers, postcards, stamp booklets and postal stationery, present special problems to the collector. When only a few of these items are relevant to a collection they can often be incorporated into a normal album. Often, however, they form collections in their own right, it may then be better to house them independently in one of the many albums designed for the purpose. These are generally available to house covers, postcards and booklets. They are usually manufactured with peg or ring-fittings but contain leaves made from a transparent material welded into pockets to fit the items they are intended to contain.

Cover album leaves are manufactured in two main types: those made from polythene and a more expensive kind made from a stiffer transparent material. The leaves usually

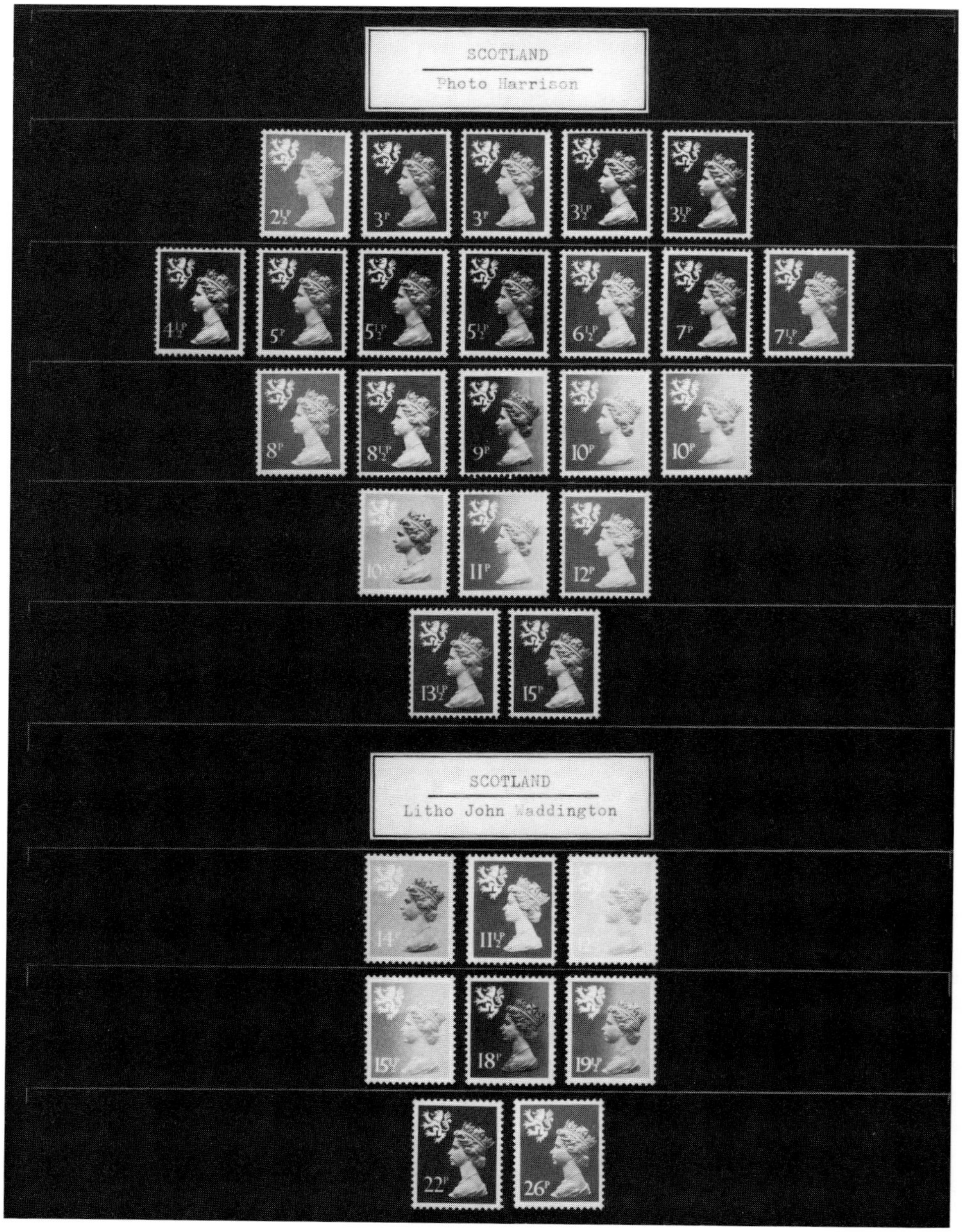

5 A stock-book page. These are ideal for storing continuing definitive series, as here, until all the stamps have been issued and can be mounted on normal album leaves; writing-up is provided by labels. Leaves are available with varying numbers of strips to facilitate different arrangements

contain one or two pockets holding, respectively, two or four standard size covers back to back. Large size pockets are also available to take abnormal sized envelopes. Each pocket contains a thin card, usually black, on which the cover may be mounted. Many of these pockets have their openings at the side nearest the spine of the album. This necessitates the removal of leaves from the album when covers are added or removed. There is also the danger of covers, unless they are securely mounted on the insert cards, sliding from the pocket into the spine of the album and becoming damaged; of greater safety and convenience are the leaves with pocket openings at the top.

Postcard albums are similar in pattern to cover albums, transparent leaves being available to hold varying numbers of postcards. The pockets are usually designed to take one of the two standard postcard sizes – 'Golden Age' (140 × 85 mm) or 'Continental' (150 × 105 mm). They are also available to take the Post Office issued 'PHQ' cards. In some postcard albums the pockets contain insert cards on which details of the postcards may be written if desired. Where pockets do not contain insert cards, postcards may be placed in them back to back or singly so that both picture and stamp sides of a card may be seen.

Booklet album leaves are available with several sizes of pocket to accommodate the most popular stamp booklet sizes, including one to show folded booklet types in an open position so that both cover and stamps can be seen.

Stock-book type albums are popular with some collectors as they enable stamps to be arranged without the need for stamp hinges or protective mounts. The album consists of a binder, usually ring-fitting, containing card leaves with horizontal transparent strips attached by their lower edge. The stamps are slipped behind the strips where they are held securely in place. The leaves are available in black or white and with strips on one or both sides. The number of strips per page varies from one to seven, enabling a wide range of stamp sizes, and even blocks and covers, to be accommodated. The scope for arrangement on these pages is not as wide as that afforded by a conventional leaf, writing-up, too, has its limitations and the problem it presents is best overcome by the use of small slips of paper inserted in the strips alongside the stamps.

Stock-book albums are not ideal for storing a large collection, they do not give the necessary scope required. They are, however, suitable for a small side-line collection or for storing stamps, such as current definitives, in some sort of order, and with some flexibility, until they are ready to be more permanently mounted.

LOOKING AFTER YOUR COLLECTION

When you have your album, treat it properly. Most spring-back albums will hold a larger number of leaves than is supplied with them, but if you put too many in you weaken the grip of the springs and eventually the metal will be strained and can snap. There is also the danger of an overfilled album disgorging its leaves when opened, or, worse, still, while being carried, with consequent damage to the stamps upon them. Albums with pegs or rings will not close properly if overloaded.

It should be remembered that an album will be much bulkier when the leaves have stamps mounted upon them, especially if the stamps are in protective mounts; covers and stamp booklets add even more bulk. If an album's binder does not close properly, or pages in a ring album will not turn easily, it will be necessary to remove some leaves and place them into another binder. Finally, do not use, in any loose-leaf album, leaves which were not intended for it.

Stamp albums should be stored vertically on shelves, not stacked lying on their backs, which places undue pressure on the stamps as well as straining the binding mechanisms. Albums which have slip-in cases obviously store very well, but with a little care (and the use of bookends if necessary) a series of volumes not in cases can be made to stay neatly upright. Different colours of binder are available for most makes of album, and use can be made of this to distinguish different countries or sections of a collection. The spines can be numbered for identification or have country names added with Indian ink, gummed labels or transfer lettering.

Try to avoid shelving albums where they will be subjected to a lot of direct sunlight or extremes of temperature. Avoid, too, storing them against the outside walls of the house. A study or bedroom is a preferable location to a living room. Flick over the pages of each album now and then, replacing at once any stamps which may have come adrift and making sure that the album is not being exposed to any dampness. Remove immediately any stamps which show signs of staining ('foxing') as this can spread to other items in the collection.

PART 2

Preparing and mounting the collection

PREPARATION

It is an axiom that, unless it is of special significance, a damaged, very heavily postmarked, or otherwise unsightly specimen should not find a place in the album. It is essential, for appearance sake, that paper, hinges, etc, adhering to the backs of stamps, should be removed before they are mounted. You may wish to display stamps on their original covers, these should be clean and without heavy creasing or tears. There are also occasions when, though the whole cover is not required, it is necessary to include a portion of the envelope as well as the stamp, in order to show a postmark or other feature, in such instances the paper should be trimmed to a neat rectangle, clear of the stamp and whatever else it is desired to show.

There are occasions when the appearance of a grubby-looking cover or stamp can be improved. It is recommended, however, that before attempting any improvements, especially if the item is at all valuable, tests are carried out on less valuable pieces in order to gain experience of the techniques required, if in any doubt leave well alone.

The most common defects likely to be found on covers are grubbiness and grease marks, tears, creases and, especially on modern items, adhesive tape. Grubby marks can often be removed with a soft pencil eraser or a piece of bread. This should be done with great care; hold the item firmly and rub gently outwards from the centre to the edges. Grease marks can sometimes be removed by placing the piece between sheets of clean dry white blotting-paper and pressing gently with a medium warm iron. Creases, too, may be treated with a warm iron and blotting-paper, though this should be dampened before use – make sure that any ink markings on the cover will not be affected. Tears, if on a piece, can often be removed by trimming it to a smaller size, when this is not possible, or the tear is on a cover, it can be repaired by pasting a piece of thin paper to the back of the item. A good quality clear paste should be used, avoid gums that may stain and never use any form of contact adhesive or transparent adhesive tape. Care should be taken when repairing the front of an envelope not to paste it to the back. Use the paste sparingly and remove any excess before it has time to dry. Before the repair has fully dried the tear may be closed by pressing it with a smooth surface (such as a finger nail or pen top) through a sheet of thin paper.

Transparent adhesive tape presents special problems to the collector. If left intact it will, in time, stain the cover and the adhesive will seep around the edges of the tape causing a mounted cover to adhere to the album page or, worse, another cover. It should, then, be removed. Tape is most easily removed with benzine or lighter fuel. Dampen the affected area with the liquid, using it sparingly to avoid staining the cover, wait a moment or two for the adhesive to loosen its hold, then carefully lift the edge of the tape and peel it away from the paper. If the tape does not come away easily do not force it, apply some more benzine and try again. Remove any traces of adhesive that may be left on the cover by dabbing it with a soft cloth moistened with benzine. If the tape covers a stamp extra care needs to be taken as many modern stamps are not colour fast in benzine. It may be better in such circumstances to try and remove the tape by using a hot iron or by exposing it to some other source of dry heat, such as a hair dryer. The tape should be carefully peeled away as the heat softens the adhesive. This is likely to be a slow process requiring great patience.

Having carried out any necessary improvements covers can, and if flimsy should, be stiffened with a piece of thin white card or stiff paper cut to size and carefully inserted.

There are also permissible actions that may be taken to improve a stamp's appearance. It may be given a good bath in warm or cold water, after first ascertaining that its colours are fast. Stamps printed on 'chalky' papers, or in aniline and certain other colours, do not like water, and will be ruined if introduced to it. Stamps with gum should not, of course, be given this treatment! Grease stains and creases in stamps may be removed by the methods applied to covers, though stamps in which the surface ink has cracked are beyond help.

The very cautious use of hydrogen peroxide will cause stamps whose colours have changed by oxidisation to revert to their pristine hues. Early stamps printed in red or orange and some blues are particularly susceptible to this change, turning to brown or black in many instances. A simple apparatus for the safe application of hydrogen peroxide can easily be made out of two small shallow trays and a piece of perforated cardboard. The bottom tray holds peroxide, just enough to cover the bottom and diluted to 10 volumes, while the top tray placed upside down acts as a lid and concentrates the vapour. The perforated cardboard which should be sandwiched between the trays holds the stamp in the vapour and out of contact with the liquid, which would dissolve the gum of mint stamps. The action may take up to twenty-four hours depending on the depth of oxidisation but the stamp should be examined from time to time to prevent over-action and bleaching.

To remove stamps from adherent paper a soak in warm water is needed, remembering that only those printed in fast colours may be so treated. A safer, though much slower, method is to float the stamps face upwards on the surface of the water, removing them when their backing paper has been soaked but before the stamps themselves have come to harm. Great care is needed when removing the stamps from their paper – a damp stamp is fragile – if there is any sign of sticking the stamp should be returned to the water, attempting to remove it may result in a tear or thin. It should be noted that the adhesives used on modern stamps are very tenacious, a longer period of soaking or floating will be required. If preferred, stamps may be placed face upwards on damp white blotting-paper or a damp sponge and the process watched with equal care. A handy home-made gadget consists of a shallow plastic tray nearly filled with a pad of blotting-paper which can be dampened as required. Any stamps on coloured paper that may not be fast in water should be dealt with separately. Having removed the stamps from their backing paper, and having made sure that no traces of adhesive remains on their backs, place them between sheets of clean white blotting-paper to dry. A light weight on top of the blotting-paper – a book is ideal – will help the stamps to dry flat. Hinges on the back of mint stamps may be removed by moistening with a fine-tipped paintbrush, ensuring that no water touches the stamp's gum. If several layers of hinges have accumulated they will have to be removed a layer at a time.

One problem that may face the collector, especially with an old collection, is that of foxing – tiny brown spots on the surface of a stamp, usually at the edges, that may spread to cover or album leaf – caused by an airborne fungus. If such a condition is suspected expert advice should be sought for it will soon spread if not checked; the use of a 10% solution of Chloramine T (BP) can help. Infected leaves and album binders should be discarded. As with most diseases, prevention is better than cure, and the condition can be kept at bay through proper storage of your collection, which should be kept dust and moisture free and be frequently aired.

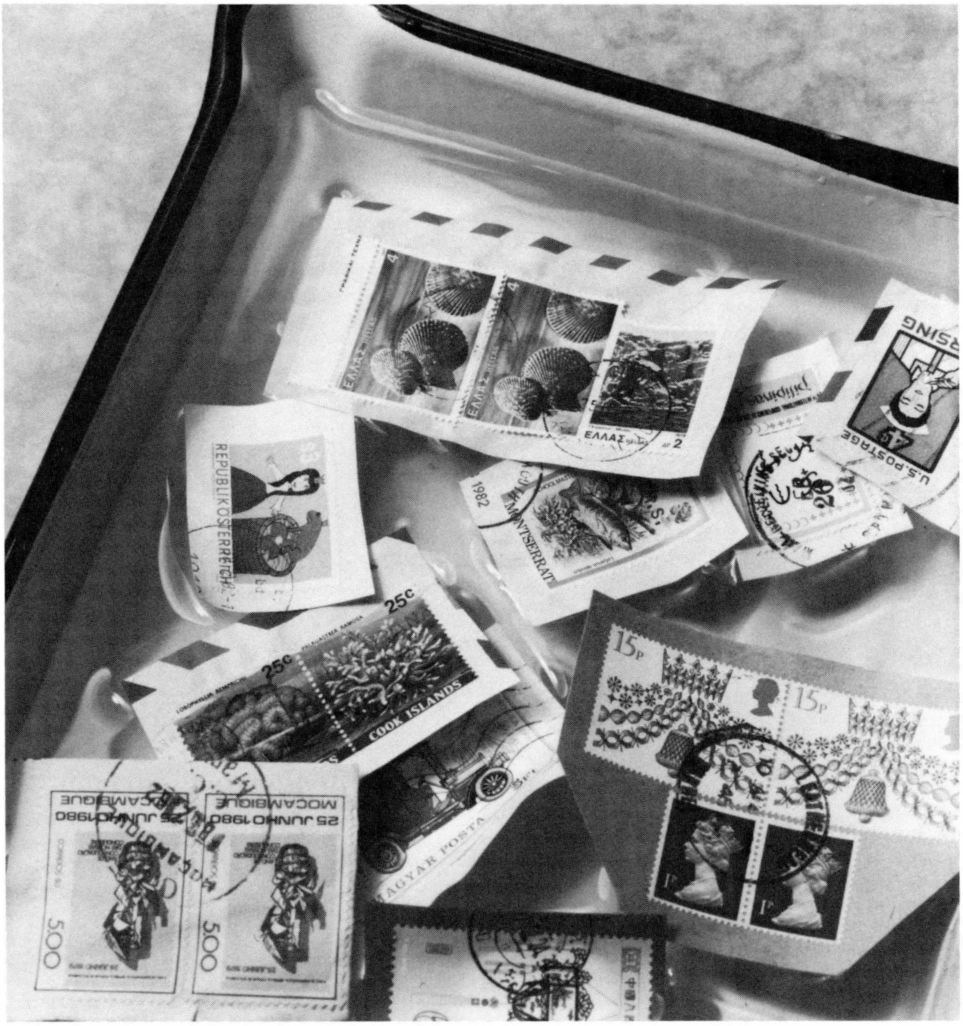

1 **Floating used stamps to remove them from their backing paper**

Having prepared your stamps and covers ready for the album the next step is to consider the best method of affixing them to the album page.

MOUNTING

In order to protect your stamps and to preserve their condition and value, it is essential to attach them to the album page in a manner which will expose them to the least possible damage. There is no excuse for false economy in this respect as good quality stamp hinges are relatively inexpensive and do very little damage to stamps. Provided that the hinges are thoroughly dry they can be removed from stamps or from album pages and leave only the tiniest mark.

In the opinion of many modern collectors however, hinging, even if infrequent, is to be avoided, especially on mint stamps, as they consider the disturbance of the gum undesirable, such mounting often reducing a stamp's resale value by a considerable amount.

Methods of mounting without hinges have become sufficiently perfected to be acceptable to the collector and economical enough to be used on a large scale. Indeed, the cost of protective mounts may be considered as recoverable by the higher market value which results from the preservation of mint stamps in unmounted condition.

HINGES

A stamp should be hinged on to a page in such a way that it can be removed from the album yet leave the page unmarked; so that the hinge can be removed from the stamp with only the faintest trace; so that the stamp can be turned over freely for the back or the watermark to be examined without bending the stamp or its perforations in any way; and so that the hinge is not visible when the stamp is placed in the album. The use of good quality peelable hinges will fulfil the first of these two conditions, but to satisfy the latter two the hinge must be applied to both stamp and album page in the proper manner. Stamps should always be handled using tweezers; this prevents damage from dirt or perspiration on the fingers. The best way to hinge stamps is shown in the accompanying illustrations, and in accordance with the following description (if using ready-folded hinges stage 1 may be ignored).

1. Holding the hinge with gummed side downwards between the thumb and forefinger of the left hand, fold about a third of its length with the tweezers, press the crease down with the thumb.
2. With the stamp face downward on the table moisten the top third of the hinge and place it in position at the top of the stamp close to the edge but clear of the perforations, taking care that the hinge is in a central position so that no part of it projects beyond the sides.
3. Hold the stamp with the tweezers, using one point of the tweezers to keep the hinge clear of the back of the stamp. The bottom of the hinge can then be slightly touched with the tongue without danger of moistening the stamp at the same time.
4. Hold both the stamp and the hinge with the tweezers (towards the top to avoid the moistened gum) and place in position on the album page. By holding the hinge against the stamp it is prevented from sticking to the page before the desired position is reached.

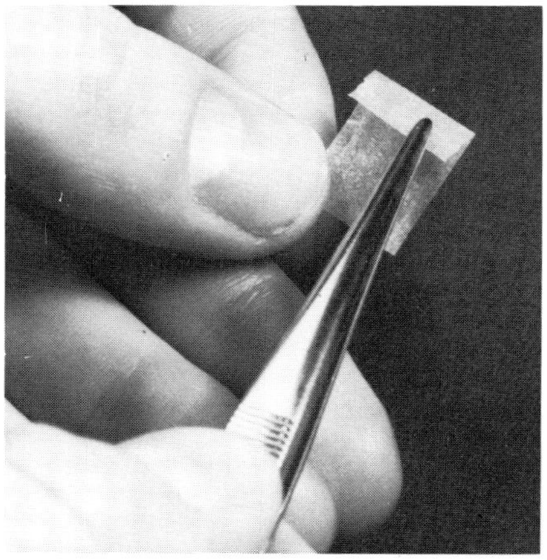

2a Using a stamp hinge. Fold over a third of the hinge . . .

2b . . . place the moistened part at the top of the stamp . . .

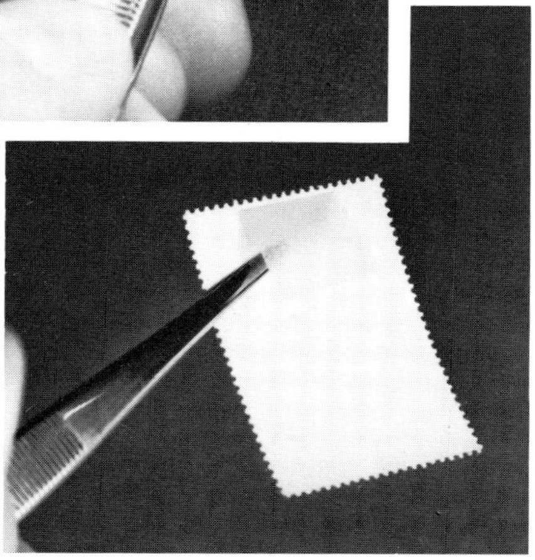

2c . . . wet only the lower part of the free end of the hinge . . .

2d . . . and place the stamp in position on the album page

It is particularly important to moisten only the lower end of the free part of the hinge, so that when mounted in the album the stamp can be turned back without creasing the top perforations. If the whole hinge is stuck to the page, it is impossible to turn up the stamp without damage and there is more likelihood of damaging the album when the stamp is removed. If the hinge has been placed in the wrong position on stamp or album page it is essential to wait until the gum is thoroughly dry before attempting to remove it; failure to do so will result in a damaged stamp or leaf.

When hinging very small stamps make sure that the hinge, even when folded, is not larger than the stamp to which it is to be applied. If the hinge is too large cut it down with scissors before using it.

Triangular and diamond-shaped stamps often present difficulties for the novice. They are correctly mounted by placing a hinge on one of the two upper sloping sides (usually the side at the top left), not across the point at the top, which will cause damage to the stamp if it is lifted for examination.

An important consideration is the amount of moisture to be applied to the hinge. This should be the minimum possible which allows the hinge to stick properly, as a very wet hinge is bound to deteriorate the stamp or mark the album page. It is of the utmost importance that no moisture should touch the back of mint stamps when the hinge is being affixed. It is not uncommon to see collections in which many of the mint stamps are stuck fast to the album leaves due to the gum on the backs being touched by moisture during mounting. Such carelessness can reduce the value of a collection very considerably.

When mounting pairs or blocks of stamps it is open to question whether the procedure adopted by some collectors of attaching the hinge to one stamp only, or in the centre and close to the upper edge, is wise. The object of attaching the hinge to one stamp only is to avoid possible damage to the gum of two stamps. Placing the hinge at the top of a block of four certainly enables the back of the stamps to be examined easily, but leaves it insecurely attached to the page, and when the leaves are turned it too often happens that the stamps turn up or over and get badly creased. Pairs should be mounted with a hinge on one of the two stamps, not with a hinge applied across the dividing perforation. On blocks the smaller portion of the hinge is best attached to the lower portion of the upper stamps so that the whole block is held firmly in place. Large blocks and strips of stamps will require hinges on two or more stamps if they are to remain secure in the album.

If hinged stamps are likely to require frequent mounting as album pages are rearranged it is possible to overcome the damage this might cause to mint stamps by hinging the stamp to thin paper. This, cut to size, is then hinged to the album leaf; any rehinging is carried out on to the backing paper, the stamp remaining fixed. This method has the disadvantage of adding extra thickness to the page, and allowance needs to be made to prevent album binders from bulging.

PROTECTIVE MOUNTS

If hinges are not acceptable protective mounts offer a satisfactory solution. These consist of a strip of clear plastic welded to a black or transparent backing strip. They come in two types, those sealed on one side only, and those sealed on two opposite sides, the centre of the backing strip being slit to allow insertion of the stamp. Both types have adhesive on the back which is moistened to affix the mounts to the album page. With the double-sealed type, only the top half should be moistened and fixed to the leaf. The bottom half remains free. This half should be lifted and the stamp pushed in as far as it will go. If the mount is then allowed to flip back into place the stamp will be held securely.

Both types come in strips of various heights which may be cut to length or cut to size to fit many standard size stamps. Sizes are indicated in millimetres and give the maximum size of the stamp that will fit the mount. The double-sealed mounts are only suitable for the sizes of stamp indicated, though they do hold the stamp more securely. The single-sealed type are more flexible. They may be cut to fit smaller stamps if the mount is too large (a border of about 2 mm should surround the stamp), thus one size of strip may be used to mount stamps of several sizes. Items which are taller than the deepest protective mount available may be mounted using two strips. For example, an item 100 mm deep may be mounted with two 55 mm strips, one at the top and one at the bottom. The strips are joined at the back with a small offcut of the gummed backing or a piece of gummed paper.

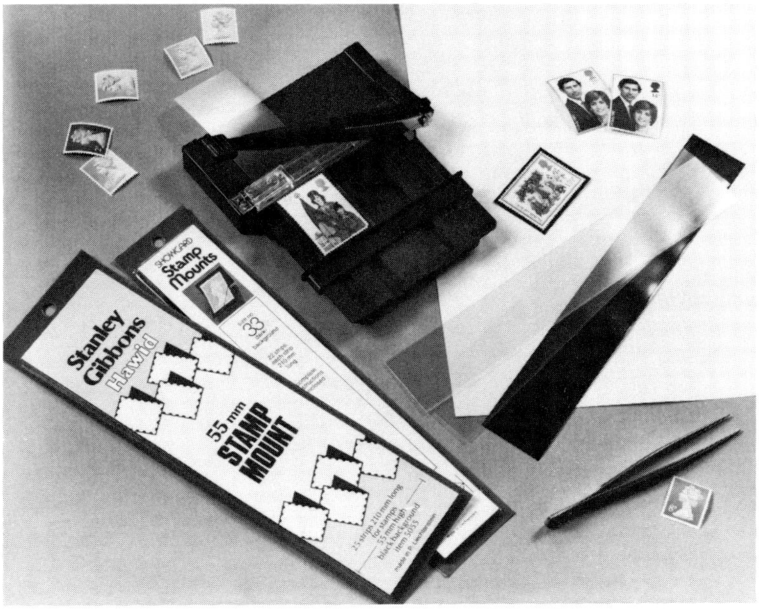

3 (*left*) Protective mounts are available in black and clear forms. A small guillotine makes cutting strips to size a quick and accurate process

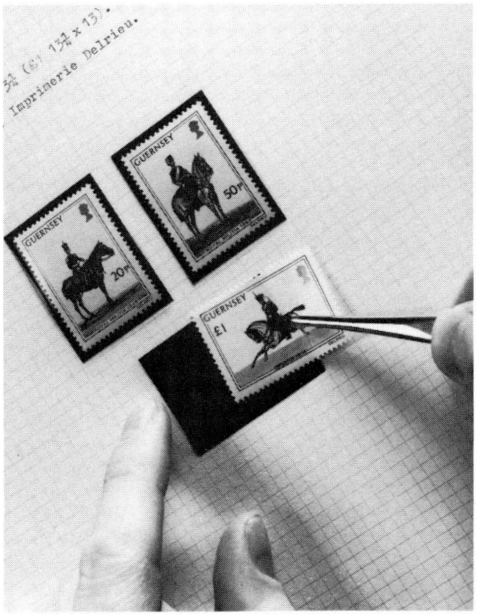

4 (*right*) Inserting a stamp into a single-sealed mount

The protective mount can then be affixed to the page in the normal way, by moistening the gum along the welded edges. On the front the two strips will overlap slightly, preventing the item inside from slipping out.

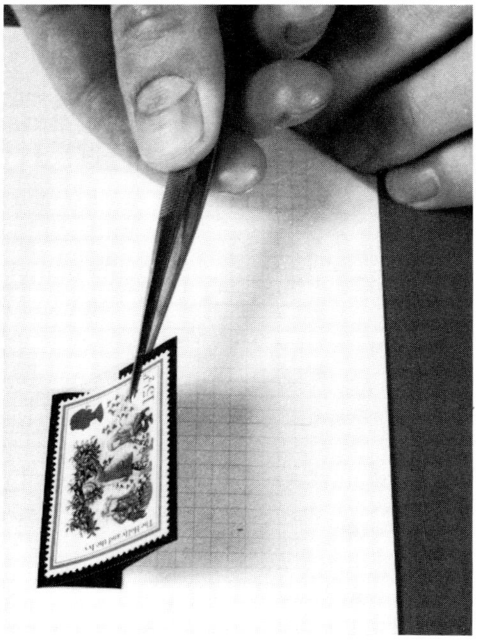

5 Using a double-sealed protective mount

6 Two strips can be overlapped to mount large pieces and hold them securely

When attaching protective mounts to the album page be careful not to apply too much moisture as there is the danger that some will seep inside the mount. Bulky items should not be placed inside mounts as pressure when the album is closed will eventually split the mount along the weld.

MOUNTING COVERS AND BOOKLETS

Covers (or postcards) may be included within a collection of stamps by mounting them with photograph corners. The small type are usually suitable, though the self-adhesive kind are best avoided; occasionally these may be difficult to attach, especially if the item is bulky, the large size mounts available from philatelic suppliers should overcome any problems.

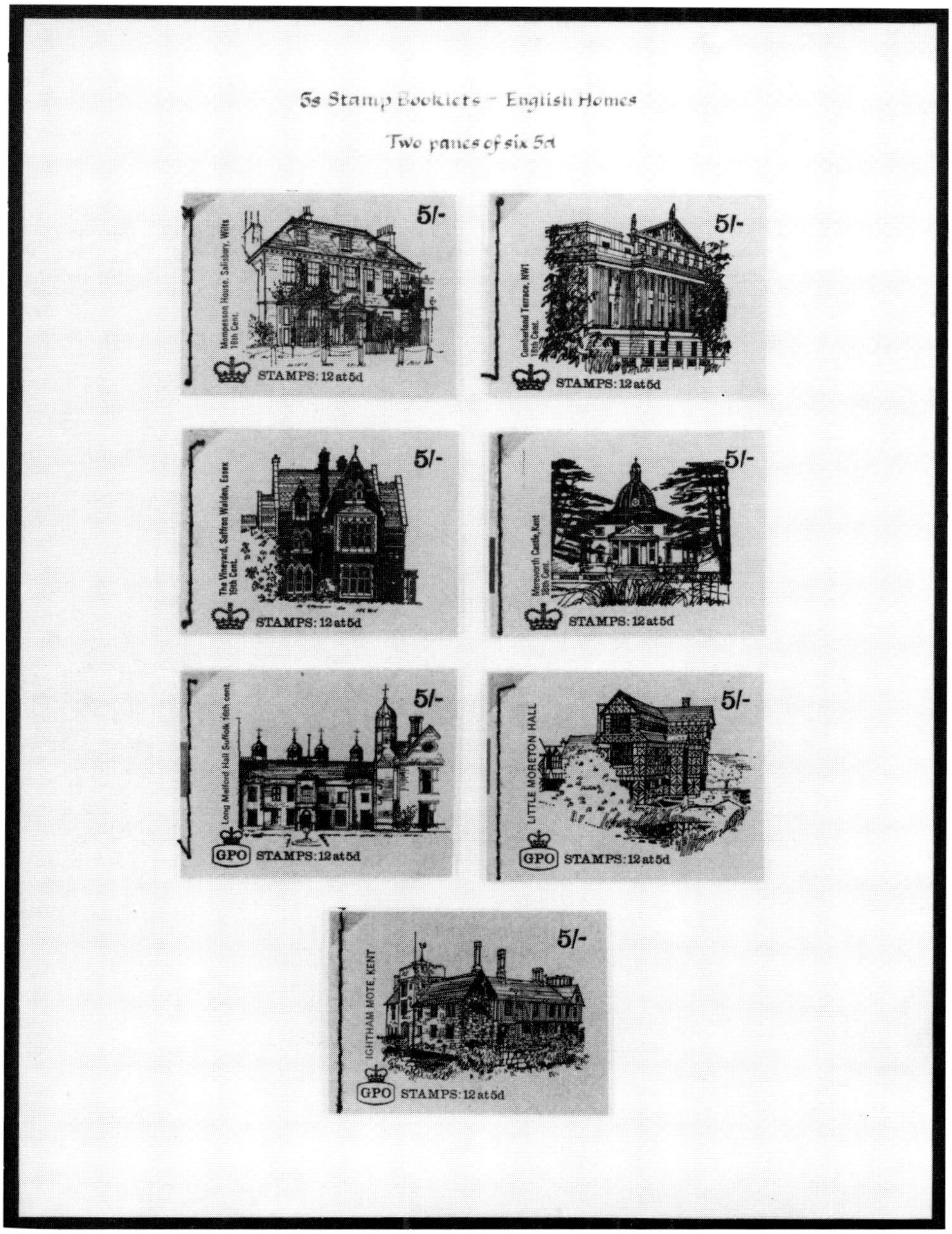

7 A page of stamp booklets mounted with photograph corners. The front edge of the back cover of each booklet is held in place by a single corner at bottom right (hidden) enabling the contents to be examined

Usually two photograph corners, at diagonally opposite corners of the cover or card, are sufficient to secure the item to the page, but if the piece is very large or flimsy four may be better.

Stamp booklets provide a different mounting problem as it may be desired to examine their contents. They may be displayed 'exploded' on the page, that is, separated into their individual panes and then mounted up separately along with the front and back covers and any advertisement or information pages. But this does tend to diminish their value and if it is wished to retain the booklet intact another method has to be found. An alternative method that enables the contents to be examined is to cut two parallel slits in the album page (use a sharp knife and a metal rule), a fraction taller than the height of the booklet, through which the back cover can be slipped. However, there is the danger with this method that the booklet may slip out and be damaged. Photograph corners can also be used to mount booklets, though they will not permit easy examination of the contents. Modern folded booklets can be flattened out and displayed intact using a protective mount if the booklet cover is not too thick.

Remember that covers and booklets are much heavier than stamps and should be mounted on a heavy-grade leaf; they may cause the album leaves to come away from the binding, especially in peg and ring-fitting albums, and these should be strengthened with reinforcement rings. Many covers or booklets in an album will, because of their bulk, reduce the number of leaves that can be held. Spacers may be required in the binding mechanism to prevent the leaves from splaying out; narrow strips of thick card, punched to fit and placed at suitable intervals, should overcome this problem. If a large number of such items are to be displayed it may be better to house them separately in a purpose-built cover or booklet album.

PART

3 Writing-up

There are various ways of actually putting your 'writing-up' on to the album page; the method chosen will depend on individual taste and ability. Many people have neat and perfectly legible handwriting that will be quite suited to writing-up their collection. Others may feel that their stamps deserve something better than their normal, perhaps untidy, handwriting and, with practice, it is possible to cultivate an acceptable standard of 'calligraphic' lettering. For those who lack the ability to produce a neat hand various mechanical means – typewriter, stencils, dry-transfer lettering – are available.

There are several reasons why a very high standard of everyday handwriting is not a prerequisite for being able to produce a neatly written-up collection. The printed squares on the pages of a blank album provide a useful visual frame on which to standardise the sizes of lettering used. Often only one or two lines of description are required and the writer does not have to produce large paragraphs of uniform writing. A good fountain-pen (filled with black ink) should be used, never a ballpoint or felt-tip pen, as this gives more control over the lettering. With some careful thought and a good deal of practice on old discarded leaves, a neat writing-up style should be within the capability of almost any collector, even if the skills of copperplate or italic scripts are beyond reach.

For those who aspire to greater things more specialised equipment will be necessary.

INK

Two kinds of ink are recommended: Indian ink and ordinary black ink. The kind to use will depend on the work to be done. For sketches, frame-lines, arrows, etc, a good Indian ink is the best and is also good for block lettering or any lettering in which there are no very fine upstrokes. For copperplate or any lettering containing hairline strokes Indian ink will be found too thick and a more fluid kind will have to be used. The colour should always be black or near black; blue or other coloured ink will clash with the variegated colours of the stamps. No particular advantage is to be gained from using a waterproof ink, a collection should not be exposed to rain or damp.

PENS

The type of pen to use will depend on the style of lettering that has been chosen. A pointed nib, which makes a line of varying thickness, depending on the pressure applied, will be required for copperplate writing. A nib with a turned-up point will be suitable for any lettering requiring no fine lines, such as block lettering or other styles referred to as 'printing'. Two or three different sizes of nib should meet most needs.

For roundhand, Gothic and Old English writing the nib has its business end cut off square or obliquely so that it draws a fine line only in a lateral direction; with an upward or downward movement and without pressure a thick line is obtained equal to the width of the pen. It is a feature of such pens that no pressure should ever be used, so that the thick strokes always remain constant for a given direction. They are made in a number of sizes, depending on the width of the writing edge. The size to use is determined by the size of the writing required; this should be approximately a fifth of the height of small letters. Such nibs may be obtained from art supply shops on cards bearing ten to twelve different sizes of nib, a penholder and ink reservoirs that may be attached to any of the nibs – sometimes the reservoir may be an integral part of the penholder. When fitting a reservoir to the pen it should be adjusted so that the point of the pen projects a millimetre or two beyond the tip of the reservoir. A No. 5 or $5\frac{1}{2}$ size nib will be found to be the most suitable for the general description of a collection, while a No. $3\frac{1}{2}$ or 4 will produce good-sized letters for headings. Of course, personal taste and practice will determine the sizes to be selected, which once adopted, should be retained throughout the work in order to maintain uniformity.

1 Pens (top to bottom): penholder with square-cut nib and reservoir; penholder with attached reservoir; penholder with pointed nib; fountain-pen with square-cut nib; ruling pen; draughtsman's pen. Nibs (left to right): pointed nib; nib with turned-up point; three square-cut nibs; two interchangeable fountain-pen nibs

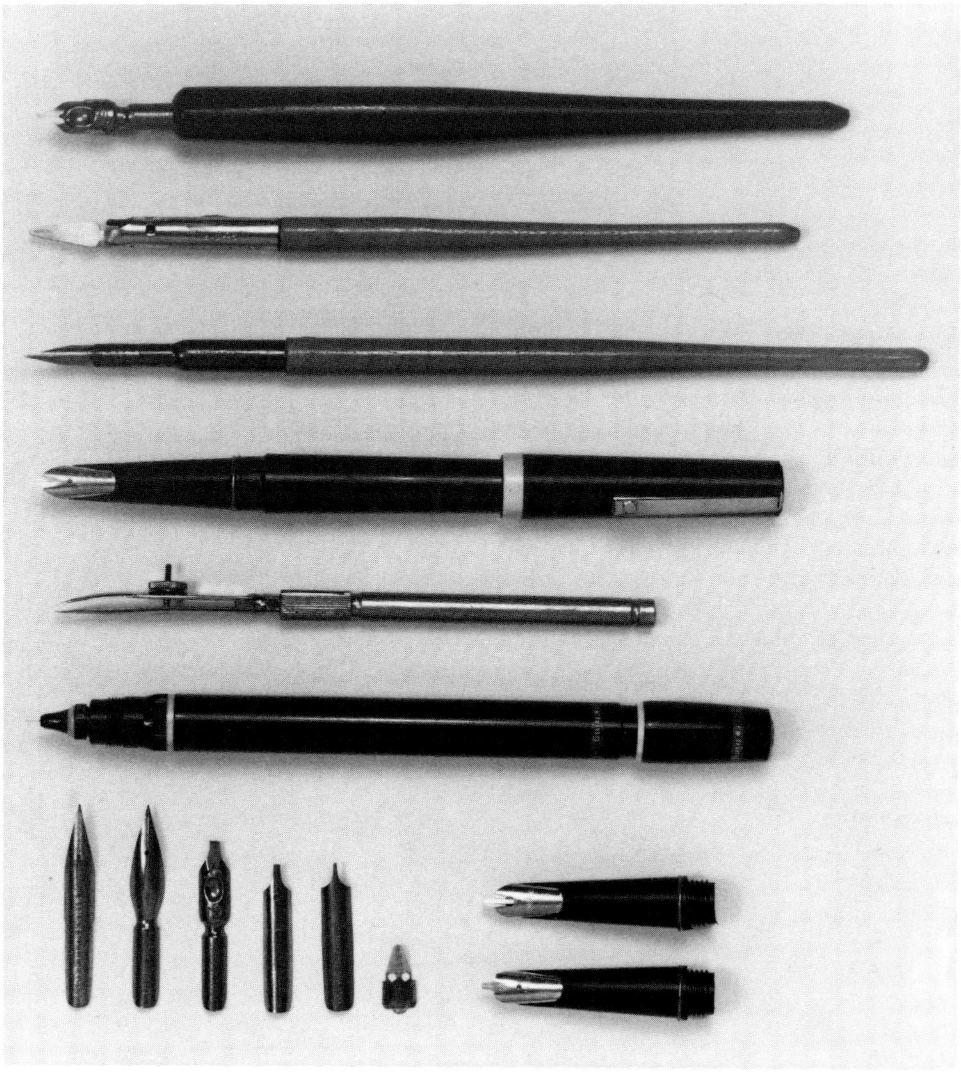

With all these pens it is advisable to use ordinary ink, although the square nibs may, if a heavier style of writing is required, be used with Indian ink, but this ink must be placed in the reservoir – use the ink filler fixed to the bottle top – and not allowed to run down inside the pen. Always test the nib on scrap paper after filling and before applying it to the album page to ensure that the ink flow is not too heavy.

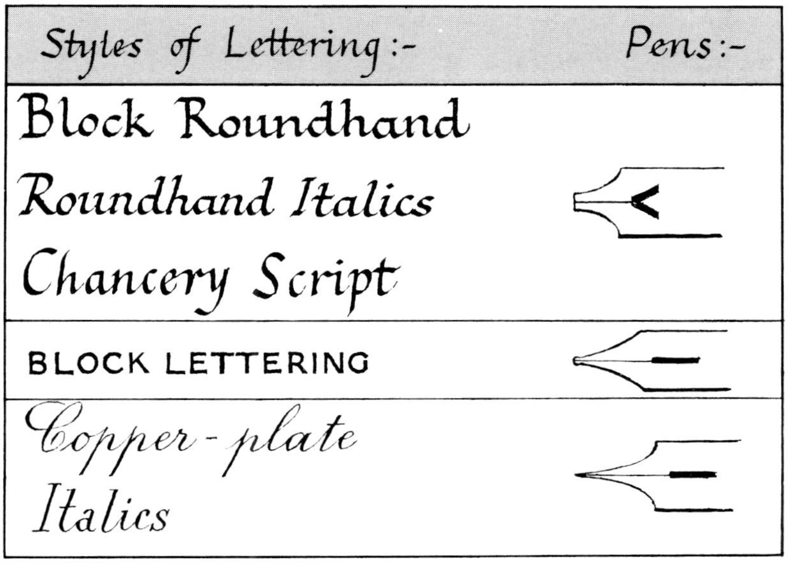

2 Styles of lettering and the nibs required

FOUNTAIN-PENS

The pens described above will require frequent filling and this, if there is a large amount of writing to do, can become rather tedious; it may also produce an uneven density in the written work. These disadvantages may be overcome by using a fountain-pen fitted with a suitable nib. Interchangeable nib units, pointed, square, oblique, right- or left-handed are available for any style of writing. Sets specifically for calligraphic writing, containing a pen and several different sizes of nib unit, are available from art suppliers and large stationers. Fountain-pens should not be used with waterproof inks. If the ink used is thicker than ordinary fountain-pen ink, it is recommended that after three or four fillings the pen be filled with water and flushed a few times.

SPECIALIST PENS

For underlining or drawing frame-lines two types of pen are available, both are superior to an ordinary nib. The first is similar to a fountain-pen but with a narrow tubular nib, designed primarily for use by draughtsmen, it may also be employed with suitable lettering stencils. Different sizes are available for varying thicknesses of line, a 0.2 or 0.3 will probably be the most suitable size for the stamp collector's purpose. In use the pen is held in a vertical position and provides a perfectly even thickness of line. This pen may also be used for block lettering, though, because it needs to be held vertically, it is rather tiring to hold for long periods.

The second pen is known to draughtsmen as a 'ruling pen'. It consists of two flat springy blades – not unlike a pair of tweezers – which can be brought close together by means of a milled-edge screw. The ink should be inserted between the blades, leaving the outside quite dry so that it can be placed against a rule without fear of smearing. When the pen is set to a given width the line will remain of even thickness whatever its length.

For sketches the draghtsman's pen or any one of the pointed pens will be suitable, the size to be used depending on the fineness of the work.

CARE OF EQUIPMENT

Whatever pens you use never let the ink dry on them. Keep a jar of water and a rag by you and after every few lines of writing, or before leaving the work, dip the pen in water and clean it. This little attention – which becomes quite automatic – will repay you tenfold in obtaining those fine hairlines and clean thick lines which are the essence of a beautiful manuscript.

THE WRITER'S OUTFIT

The following list of articles should be sufficient for writing-up many volumes:

Indian ink
Ordinary black ink
Coloured ink (for underlining if desired)
Pointed pens } with holder – or
Square pens }
Fountain-pen with appropriate nibs
Ruling pen or
Draughtsman's pen
Rule
Jar of water
Rag
Blotting-paper

BLACK-LEAF ALBUMS

Although coloured leaves are best avoided (the colour may not be fast) black-leaf albums are preferred by some collectors. At first sight writing upon black paper appears to present some difficulties. It is obvious that ordinary inks are quite useless, but if the proper materials are used, it is as easy to write on black paper as on the more usual white.

Three methods of annotating black-leaf albums offer themselves to the collector: white pencil, gummed labels, pen and white 'ink.'

Little need be said about white pencils. They stand in much the same relation to black albums as ordinary pencils do to white albums; suitable perhaps for hasty notes but incapable of giving a really fine finish to a collection. Stamp collectors may, however, find them useful on account of their convenience. They are used in the same way as lead pencils, though, being generally softer, they need less pressure and more frequent sharpening. It is advisable to have a piece of sandpaper on which the exposed lead can be brought to a fine point without any flat side, to ensure strokes of even thickness.

Gummed labels may be produced with the same equipment used for writing-up white leaves. Hints on their production and use is given further on in this book.

Pen and white 'ink' possesses the same scope, the same ease of writing and the same attractiveness of finish as ordinary black on white writing-up. The pens and the manner of formation of the lettering are the same; only the medium differs. The only slight drawback is the impossibility of using a fountain-pen.

There are several kinds of white suitable for using with a pen. Process White, sold in the form of a moist paste to which water must be added for use, is the best for our purpose as it is quite finely ground. Various mixtures are sold under the name of White Ink differing from the pastes in that they are already thinned and supposedly ready for use. Waterproof White Inks are also available which are quite good.

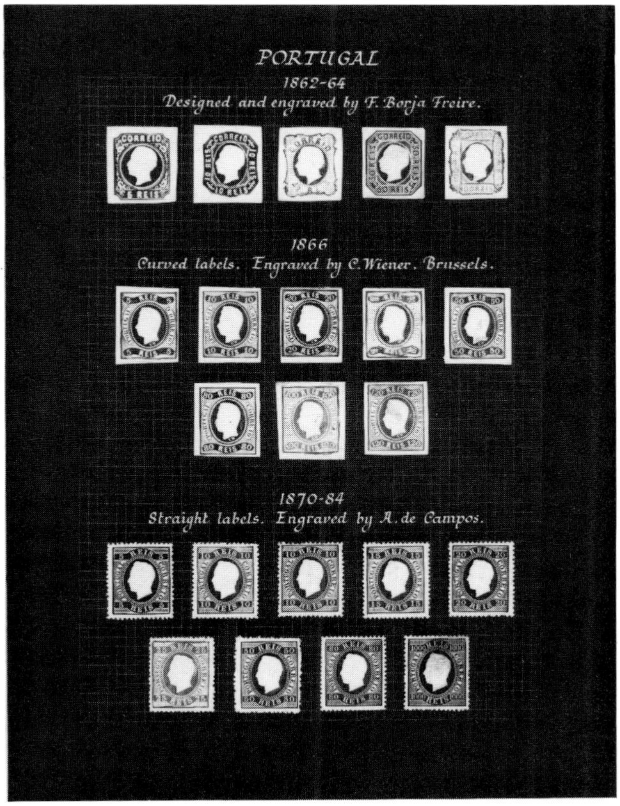

3 A straightforward collection of classic Portugal written-up in roundhand italics on a black leaf

It is most important for the satisfactory use of any of these Whites to understand how they differ in substance from the black or other coloured inks commonly used. Most black or coloured inks are dyes in solution, all the Whites consist of an insoluble white pigment mixed with water and gum, or some other liquid. With ordinary inks the pen may be dipped in the pot with the assurance of always drawing properly mixed colour. With white inks the pigment always tends to settle at the bottom and consequently the pot-dipper finds that successive dips become more watery unless, in despair, the nib is plunged to the bottom where it picks up a lump of thick sediment.

The whole secret of using any white ink successfully is to keep the pigment thoroughly mixed with the liquid medium.

The procedure to follow should be this:

1. Get together a bottle of White and whichever pens have been selected. Also a small camel-hair brush, a rag and a jar of water. Owing to the chemical action of hard water on the white pigment it is a worthwhile precaution to use distilled water for dilution to avoid the possibility of the writing becoming oxidised in the course of years. Failing this, boiled or softened water is recommended in preference to tap water.
2. Mix the contents of the bottle of White very thoroughly with a stick until no lumps are left.
3. Take a few brushfuls of White on to a saucer or artist's china pan. Again mix well with the brush and thin out by adding water with the brush. Even the so-called ready-to-use mixtures are too thick for writing and need to be thinned in this way.

4. Apply the ink with the brush to both sides of an ordinary pen or under the clip if a reservoir pen is used, and you are ready for writing.

It is not vain repetition to say again that it is just as easy to write with white ink as with black. The difficulty sometimes encountered by beginners is in trying to write with ink not sufficiently diluted or properly mixed. It is best to add too much water at first and try the result. Do not be misled by the greyish appearance of the ink whilst wet. In drying, which may take five minutes or so, it will become whiter. If it is then still too grey, wipe the pen clean, add a little more White to the mixture on the saucer, mix well with the brush, and apply it to the pen and try again. The correct mixture should flow as perfectly as from a fountain-pen and dry a brilliant white.

White ink dries on the pen more rapidly than do ordinary inks and after every three or four words the mixture on the saucer should be stirred with the brush and applied to the pen, at the same time brushing the latter in order to mix the new supply with the old. Never allow the pen to run half dry or there will be a difference in tone marking the place where the pen is replenished, which is particularly disfiguring when it happens in the middle of a word. It is better to recharge the pen at frequent intervals to make sure of a regular flow. Evaporation of the supply on the saucer is sometimes fairly rapid and should be remedied by occasional small additions of water to maintain the correct consistency. From time to time the pen should be dipped in water and wiped off completely to avoid any undesirable thickening of the lettering due to the formation of little crusts around the point. The pen should, of course, be thoroughly cleaned before being put away.

As already stated the pens required and the formation of the letters are the same as for black ink. However, in the choice of style of lettering one should be influenced by the fact that the white *quadrillé* generally appears rather more prominent on black leaves than the pale tinted *quadrillé* does on white leaves. For this reason it will probably be agreed by most collectors that on black paper the heavier styles of lettering look best. The delicate upstrokes of good copperplate writing are apt to get lost in the *quadrillé* and the lettering look spidery, although this disadvantage can be overcome by using a thicker pointed nib. One final piece of advice is that, whatever style of writing is used, the pages should always be interleaved to avoid the white ink rubbing off.

LETTERING

The choice of the style of lettering the collector is going to adopt, be it black or white, should not be made without due consideration. The question of personal fancy, which is not so very important, should be subordinated firstly to the talent of the writer, and secondly to the type of collection which is to be arranged.

Seven different styles are illustrated, belonging broadly to three groups: the first style is produced by a thick-pointed pen, the next four by square pens, and the last two by fine-pointed pens. If a little practice is carried out patiently with each type in turn, some idea will be obtained of one's ability to write with a particular pen in preference to the others. Those who have a good control of their fingers may find themselves successful with copperplate or roman italics which require a firm yet delicate touch, whilst others who like to feel some guidance from the pen will prefer to use the less flexible roundhand type, producing thick and thin strokes automatically. For those who dare not trust themselves to do a sustained curve the plain block letters will commend themselves on account of their more staccato strokes.

Some thought should also be given to the type of collection that is being written-up. The general guiding principle is that the greater the amount of writing, the less ornate it should be. If the subject is a general collection in which only the main headings appear above each issue, with a few particulars occupying three or four lines at the most, copperplate or roundhand italics may be more suitable; but if the collection requires notes under many of the stamps it will be wise to choose a more compact style, like block lettering, so that more may be written within a small space.

BLOCK LETTERING

The simplest lettering style is block capitals, because all its elements are of uniform thickness. In order to master the necessary strokes it is well to practise lettering about twice the size required in the collection. Use smooth paper, with three guide-lines ruled 6 mm apart for each line of lettering, and a pen with a good thick point. Maintain an even pressure on the pen and rest an instant at the finish of each stroke before lifting the pen, to ensure sharp terminals.

4 Plain block lettering and its basic strokes

There are ten elemental strokes which, when combined one with another, will form every letter in the alphabet. Each elemental stroke must be carried through without stopping or lifting the pen and – what is very important for perfect regularity – must always be made in the same direction. It will be seen from the illustration that this direction is downwards or sideways but never pushing up against the direction of the pen: this is a cardinal rule to observe in block and roundhand lettering. The rule does not apply to copperplate style as this is a faster writing which depends for its gracefulness more on a supple swinging movement than on deliberate strokes.

Start with vertical strokes, then oblique strokes, after which try combinations such as E, F, H, I, N, M, Z, etc. When you can make the straight strokes uniformly go on to the circular exercises with a few half-circles first to the left and then to the right. Now combine the two, forming the letter O. Follow these with the other circular letters, C, D, G, S, etc, and you will have completed the entire alphabet as illustrated.

The small letters and numerals are based on the same principles and offer no greater difficulties. Italics is the name given to all styles of lettering when they are written with a slant. Care should be taken that the inclination is always uniform.

ROUNDHAND AND CHANCERY SCRIPT

The next style shown is block roundhand and is an attractive form produced by square pens.

For practising, a fairly large-size pen should be used, giving lettering about 5 mm high, that is five times the width of the nib. The pen should be held at an angle of forty-five degrees, so that an upward stroke from left to right will be thin, while a downward stroke from left to right will yield the maximum thickness. Never apply pressure to square pens or the thick strokes will not be uniform.

The elemental strokes are approximately the same as for block lettering, but owing to the shape of the pen the resulting effect is quite different. The shape of the letters requires the use of curves and straight lines, and their construction should be carefully studied from the illustration as it does not follow what appears to be the obvious way.

5 Basic roundhand strokes

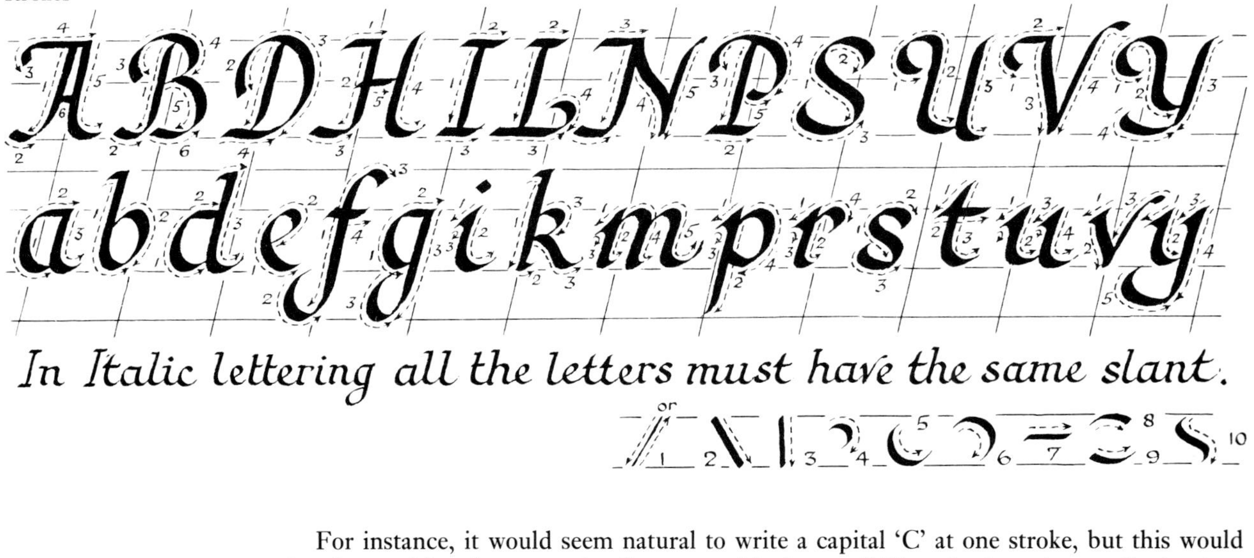

For instance, it would seem natural to write a capital 'C' at one stroke, but this would involve pushing the pen point foremost with the possibility of spluttering or digging into the paper. The better way is to form the 'C' in two strokes, each drawn downwards. The same applies to all other letters; always construct them by downward or sideways strokes regardless of the number of strokes that will be necessary.

It will at first seem impossible to connect up the component strokes without showing the join, but after a little practice there will be no difficulty in making a flawless curve. The capitals show a tendency towards block lettering, and may be used alone very effectively for the titles at the top of each page or at the beginning of a country.

The beauty of block roundhand is in its low and expanded appearance; it should not be spoilt by contracting the letters or otherwise altering the proportions shown. If a taller lettering is required in order to get more words to a line it will be better to slant the letters, thereby obtaining what are called roundhand italics. A smaller nib should be used of a width of a sixth instead of a fifth of the height of the small letters. The capitals are more elongated and made more ornate by the extension of the serifs.

6 Block roundhand

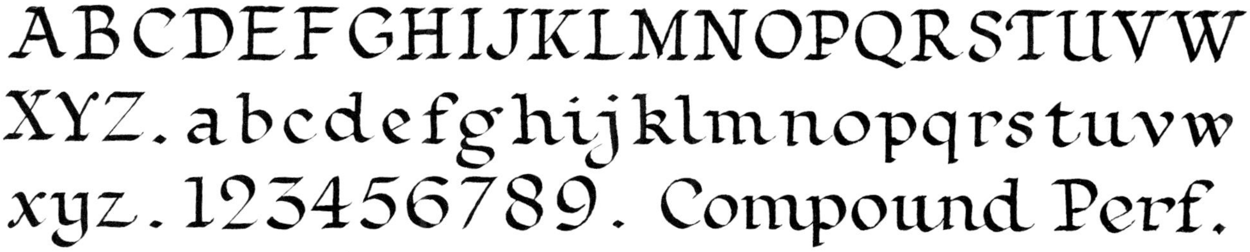

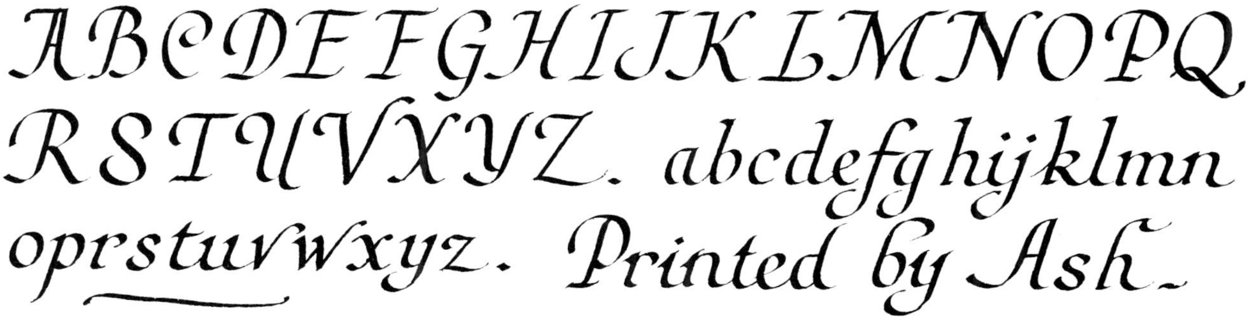

7 Roundhand italics

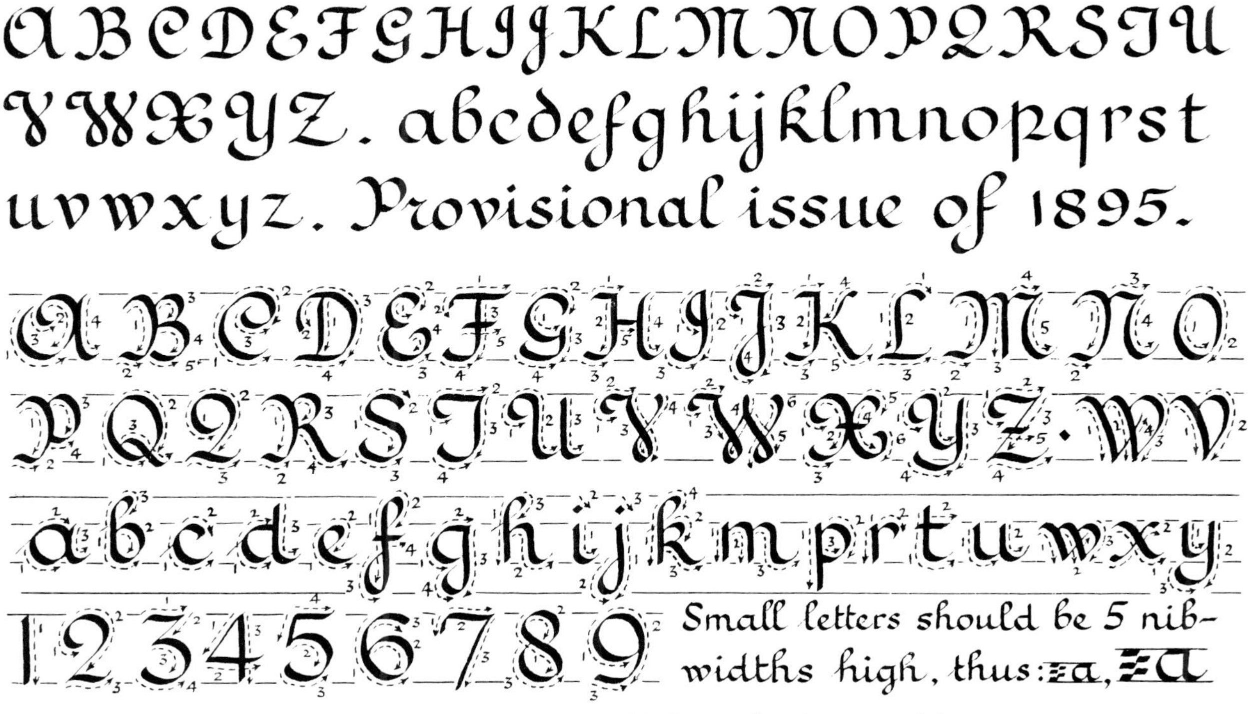

Whether you are going to write-up your collection in block roundhand or one of the other square pen styles, it is well to practise until you can obtain graceful results with the simplest before attempting the more elaborate which are derived from it.

8 An ornate roundhand style

In recent years a welcome revival and development of the sixteenth-century style of writing known as chancery script has taken place, and its eminent suitability for stamp collections brings it into this book. A great asset of this lettering for our purpose is its lesser formality and the consequent possibility of the writer introducing an individual touch to the collection. Owing to the shape of the letters and the manner of joining them together, a fair speed can be achieved with excellent legibility. An added help in this direction is the use of a fountain-pen with appropriate nib.

9 Chancery script

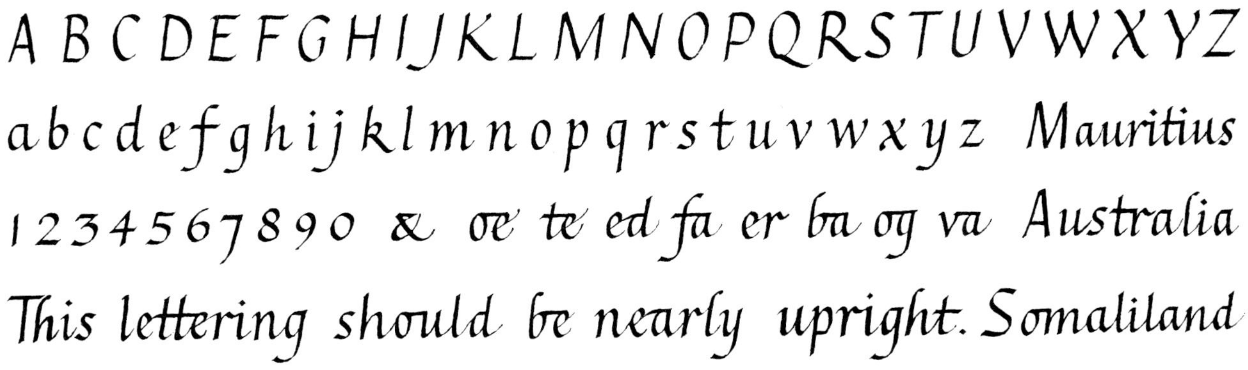

All of these square nib styles are most effective in stamp collections as they are neither too light to be readable nor so heavy as to be overpowering, and the choice of one is entirely a matter of taste.

COPPERPLATE AND ITALICS

These two scripts are produced by fine-pointed pens – and a delicate touch. The italic style illustrated is a fairly easy lettering to follow, the copperplate, with its many flowing curves may seem more daunting.

10 Copperplate and its strokes

Unfortunately, there are no secrets to be disclosed as a short cut to success. The only recommendation to be given is that a good flowing ink be used and that the pen be kept clean. Practise by writing in a size larger than would be used in a collection, and with pencilled oblique lines every centimetre to indicate the correct slant. The points to watch are a uniform inclination and an even thickness of the strokes. A rather finer surfaced paper or card is necessary than is used for other types of lettering, as the pen is apt to follow the crevices or pick up fibres of paper.

11 Italics *Issue consisting of 6 values*

With a little practice and patience you will be surprised how soon you will produce a lettering which, if not perfect in detail, is at least of quite pleasing appearance when seen in the mass. Do not be downhearted if your first efforts are not crowned with success, for only practice makes perfect, and it is certain that anyone whose hand is not hopelessly shaky can produce satisfactory writing with a little perseverance.

CORRECTING MISTAKES

If the pen produces ragged work, find out why. Is it the quality of the paper, the ink, or the pen? Remember that you cannot do clean work with a dirty pen, so clean it frequently. Going over strokes a second time usually clogs the point with crusted ink or fibres. Study the construction of each letter before you start and it will not be necessary to retrace them.

If a mistake has been made blot the wet ink as quickly as possible and leave it a few minutes to dry. If only one or two letters are wrong do not attempt to scratch them out before correcting, but, on the contrary, superimpose the correct ones over them and, when dry, scratch out the parts of the error that show with a sharp knife. In this manner the surface of the paper will not be spoilt nor result in the correction spreading. An alternative method is carefully to paint out the unwanted parts using a fine brush and paint mixed to match the paper; this method is only advisable if a waterproof ink has been used. Errors in white ink are easily obliterated with Indian ink.

TYPEWRITERS

If, after due trial, you have convinced yourself that a handwritten collection is beyond your capabilities do not despair, there are a number of alternatives open to you. Perhaps the best of these is the typewriter, even a 'one-fingered' typist will, after a short time, be able to produce a neat, and consistent, style of writing-up.

Although more expensive than pen and ink, a small portable typewriter can be bought relatively cheaply. Choice of machine is huge, and the many features available may seem bewildering, ask for a demonstration before buying and bear in mind your specialist needs. Essential points to watch are: will your album page fit the machine – take a page with you to check; does the typewriter have all the characters you are likely to need; is the typeface a suitable one – a small face may be better than a large one. Remember, too, that pages with interleaving attached are not suitable for use in a typewriter; linen-hinged leaves may also cause difficulties and produce uneven typing. Refinements that may be useful, though are not essential, include: tabulation; touch control (to vary the pressure needed on the keys); half-spacing; ability to add special keys (foreign characters, accents, etc). You may have access to, or feel it worthwhile to purchase, an electric machine. These will provide even density of typing whatever the pressure on the key, in fact, the lighter the touch the better. Sophisticated electric machines have the ability to correct errors and for the typeface to be changed. Whatever kind of machine is chosen a black ribbon should be used for typing; if the machine has facilities for a carbon ribbon this will give a much better impression than the standard, though more economical, nylon ribbon.

At first the availability of just one size and style of type that is offered by most typewriters may seem limiting. However, with careful use of capital and small letters, spacing and underlining it should be possible to provide a sufficient variety of emphasis on the album page. Capitals, possibly with a space between each letter, could be employed for country names or page headings; capitals and small letters with underlining for subheadings; and plain capitals and small letters for the main text; these are just some of the possibilities available. For large pieces of text small letters rather than capitals should be used, they are much easier to read. Each letter on a typewriter, except for some expensive machines, takes up the same amount of space. This makes it very simple to judge how much space a piece of text will take. By counting the number of letters and marking off the line length on the album page centering is made easy. 'Justification' (where all the lines of text are of equal length) can also be easily achieved; a typewriter with half-spacing facility makes this easier as lines with an uneven number of characters can be adjusted by reducing the space between words.

The new owner of a typewriter is advised to get used to the machine by practising on sheets of scrap paper before attempting to write-up expensive album pages. If a mistake has been made it may be possible to correct it, if it involves just one or two letters, by using one of the correcting fluids or correcting paper available from stationers. Typewriter erasers are likely to rub a hole in the album leaf and are best avoided. Correcting paper is rather like white 'carbon paper', it is inserted between the typewriter ribbon and the album sheet 'carbon' side down and the incorrect letter typed again. The correcting paper is then removed, the machine back-spaced, and the correct letter typed in place. Correcting fluid is used by brushing it over the error, waiting until it is dry, and then re-typing. However, after a while the fluid thickens and becomes difficult to use, making thick and unsightly blobs on the page. Too many corrected errors on a page will spoil the look of the whole leaf, under these circumstances it will be better to re-type the page concerned rather than 'spoil the ship for a hap'orth of tar'.

STENCILS

Our review of the available methods of writing-up continues by examining stencils which, though originally designed for engineers' and architects' drawings, have been adopted to some extent by stamp collectors.

These stencils consist of strips of plastic pierced with the letters of the alphabet and numerals. Each character is brought into position above the place where it is to be written and the contours of the characters are followed with a special pen which exactly fits the grooves allowing little chance of deviation. The stencils are raised from the paper by two runners which permit the stencil to be moved backwards and forwards without fear of smudging the wet ink.

The various instruments are well thought out and the method enables even the most clumsy-handed writer, after a little practice, to achieve a good effect. Though progress is rather slow if there is much small lettering to be done, there is the satisfaction of knowing that the writing will show no variation from start to finish.

A wide range of sizes and styles of lettering is available and the choice of which to use enables the collector to personalise a collection. Although the requirements of collectors may differ it is suggested that the following selection would cover the majority of collections:
Large capitals for country names
Smaller capitals for secondary headings
Small letters for descriptions

Large figures for dates and perforations
Smaller figures for catalogue numbers, fractions, etc.

Try and select a range of stencils that requires only one size of pen. This is an important point as working with several pens complicates matters in many respects. A small board with a transparent rule affixed is most useful for holding album leaves properly aligned and centred, the stencil may be slid along the rule to obtain correctly aligned letters. Very small stencils are considered too difficult to follow.

12 Stencils can provide an acceptable alternative to hand lettering

13 By doubling letters a personal touch may be given to stencil lettering

A B C D E F G H I J K L M N O P

A B C D E F G H I J K L M N O

A B C D E F G H I J K L M N

C·A·N·A·D·A I–N–D–I–A

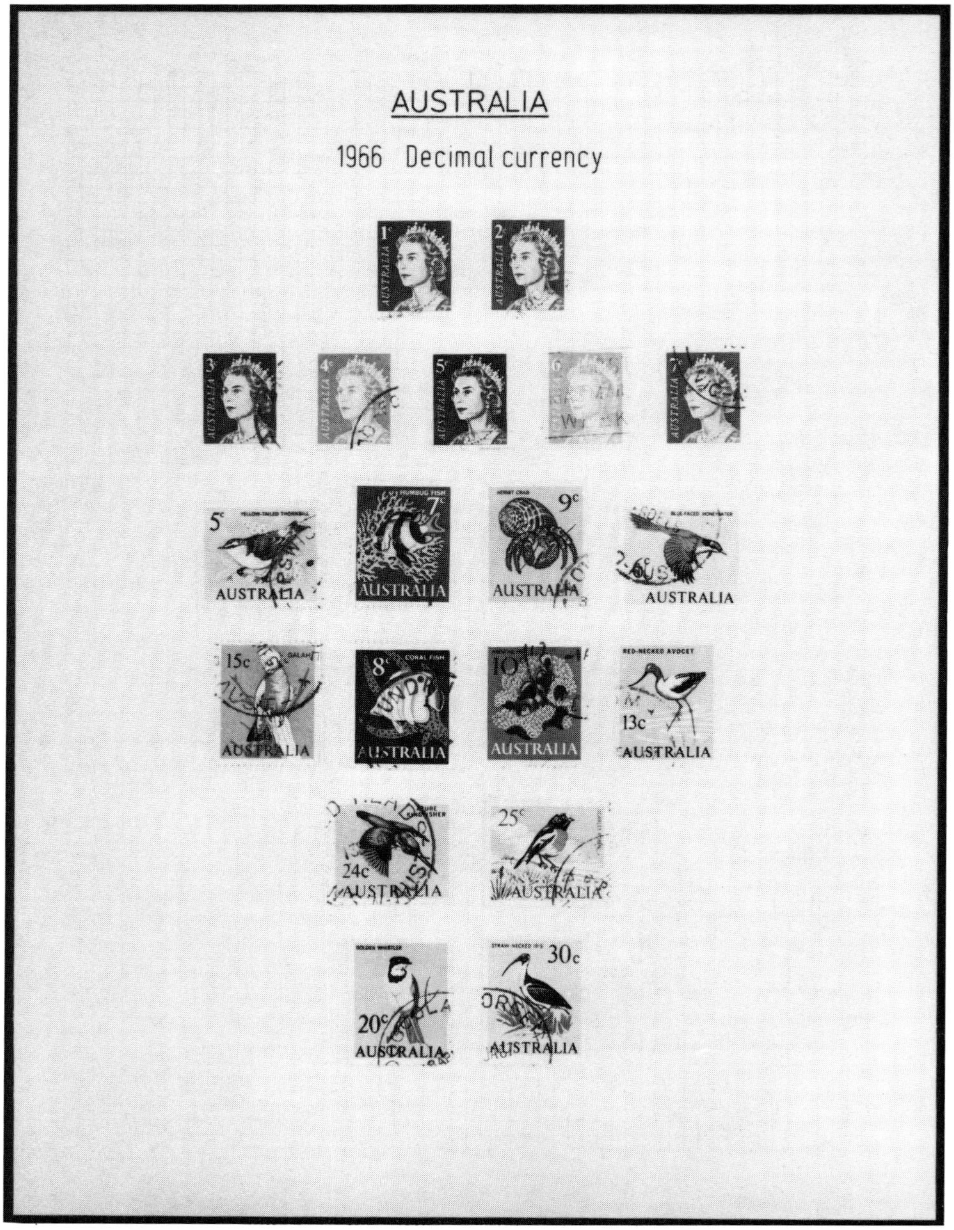

14 Stencils are time consuming to use, they are best employed where little writing-up is required, as in this simple page from a collection of Australia

For those who may object to the monotony of stencilled letters, it may be of interest to see from a few examples that, with a little ingenuity, stencils can be made to produce variations. These examples were simply made by partly doubling normal letters with additional strokes produced by shifting the stencil. A little more trouble perhaps but the result gives an individual touch which may be used, for example, for the name of the country.

DRY-TRANSFER LETTERING

A method of lettering that is finding favour with some collectors is dry-transfer lettering, originally intended for commercial artists, the method is capable of giving a finish to rival printing.

15 Using dry-transfer lettering. The backing sheet prevents accidental transfer of letters if placed between the lettering and album page. The dashes beneath the letters are used for alignment

The basic method of use is simple. The letters are printed on a transparent sheet, the required letter is placed in position and transferred to the album page by rubbing the carrier sheet over the entire area of the letter with a ballpoint pen. A little practice is required to achieve good results; letters should be properly aligned and spaced and transferred complete. To help with alignment and spacing some transfer sheets have a guide-line printed 3 mm below the letters. If a pencil line is drawn on the leaf at a point 3 mm below the required base-line of the lettering and the guide-line placed on it perfect alignment should be achieved. It will also help when transferring letters if the album leaf is attached to a board so that it does not move about.

When a line of lettering has been transferred erase the guide line taking care not to damage the lettering (protect it by covering it with the backing sheet supplied with each sheet of lettering), then, keeping the lettering covered, burnish it to the page by rubbing over it with a pen top or similar smooth object. Mistakenly transferred letters may be removed with a soft eraser or a piece of adhesive tape – again, protect the other letters with the backing sheet. A wide variety of typefaces is available in both black and white, though not all of them are suitable for use in stamp collections; consult the manufacturer's catalogue to find the most suitable. The small size of lettering that is most suited to writing-up is more difficult to transfer neatly than larger sizes; seriffed letters are more difficult to transfer than sans-serif faces as the serifs are prone to break away as the letters are rubbed down.

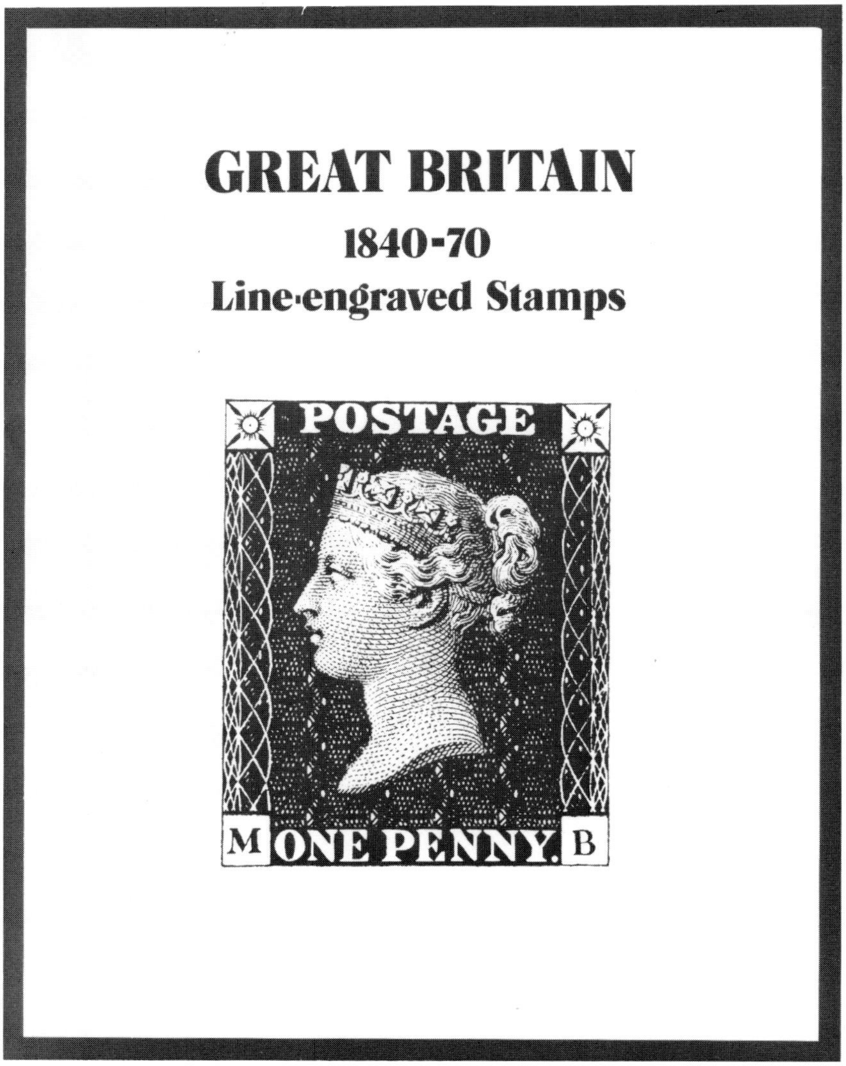

16 A title page for a collection of Great Britain produced with dry-transfer lettering and an enlarged drawing

If it is contemplated writing-up a large collection by dry-transfer lettering it is likely to be very time consuming and costly. Dry-transfer sheets contain only a limited number of each letter and one soon finds that a particular letter or number has been used up and another sheet is required. For this reason dry-transfer lettering is best used to provide headings in conjunction with another method of writing-up used for the text. Even this method must be used with care, 'AUSTRALIA', for example, lettered on every page will soon use up all the 'A' characters! A small collection with little writing-up may benefit from the use of dry-transfer lettering, and it may be worthwhile to use it for a special exhibition entry.

LABELS

One last method of writing-up remains to be discussed – the label. Gummed labels used to be available to enable collectors of British Commonwealth stamps to write-up a straightforward collection in an economical manner, now, however, they are restricted to world country names, which may be of use to the general collector.

However, labels can be made by using one of the writing-up methods already described. Such labels can be used to write-up stock-book and black album pages as well as white pages, though when used on black leaves their light colour may be felt to clash with and distract from the prime object of a stamp collection – the stamps.

Labels, even if of the same colour as the album leaf, will appear obvious to the eye when fixed in position. This effect can be lessened to some extent by, paradoxically, making it more obvious. A very thin frame line around the label or a label of a different, but not obtrusive, colour such as pale grey, can make all the difference.

The use of labels on a page should not be overdone. Three or four is ideal, though exceptions will occasionally need to be made. A page in which every stamp has a label beneath it will look ridiculous. If several stamps on a page need a description it will be better, though less convenient to read, if they are combined on one label and linked to the stamps by a code letter or number, this may be written directly on the leaf beside the appropriate stamp.

The advantages of using labels are that they avoid wastage of album pages through mistakes in lettering or typing and that they enable stamps and labels to be moved around on the page until the best arrangement has been found. If a label is of the wrong shape or size it can be remade or reworded to better fit the design. This may be especially helpful where an asymmetrical style of arrangement has been chosen, a style that may be particularly useful in a thematic collection.

17 Labels are best cut with a sharp knife and a metal rule

Labels may be affixed to the album leaf with hinges or a spot or two of paste. Two points to note when using labels are: to ensure that they are cut straight and square – use a sharp craft knife, metal rule and square or photographic print trimmer – never use scissors; and to mount them on the page so that they are all straight – if the first point has been observed the *quadrillé* on the album leaf will make this an easy task. Failure to observe these points will completely spoil the appearance of a page.

STYLE

One last point to be made applies whatever method of writing-up has been used – consistency of style. This refers to such things as the use of capital letters, abbreviations and punctuation. If you decide to use the form 'First Day Cover' in one place use it in all and do not change it to 'first day cover'; Roman numerals referring to plates or types should not suddenly become Arabic ones. Stylistic points may be extended to cover the use of spacing and the position of headings and subheadings, though these may have to be altered to accommodate different numbers and sizes of items on the page. If you are using abbreviations it should be remembered that not all of those lucky enough to see your collection will understand them, it may, therefore, be a good idea to spell out the abbreviation when it first appears, thus: 'c.d.s. (circular date stamp)'; remember not to change 'c.d.s.' to 'cds' later in the collection.

You may not remember all of the points of style you had decided on as your collection progresses and new pages are added. You may find it helpful under such circumstances to make a list of them for future reference. Even if not observed throughout a collection such stylistic details should, at least, be followed throughout a page. A sudden change of style within a short space will not only give the impression of untidy thinking, but may also be confusing to the reader if, for example, Type IV is suddenly changed to Type 4. Such details may seem of minor importance, however, they will, if observed, give your collection that extra professional touch.

PART 4 *Arrangement*

STAMPS VERSUS WRITING-UP

The great problem which faces the collector about to arrange stamps in a blank album is the extent to which they should be described in writing. It is obvious that some description is necessary, or the collection will convey nothing to those who inspect it, and may even cause confusion to its owner. On the other hand, the collection is presumably to be a collection of stamps, not a history book, or a display of its owner's artistic capabilities. The safe rule is that writing-up should be reduced to the absolute minimum consistent with expressing the intention of the collection, and that decorative effects should be confined to such as are necessary to enhance the appearance of the stamps or to emphasise the presence of special items.

Collections arranged by persons of great artistic ability, with scrolled frames to the stamps, ornate borders, and even large pictorial designs, can look very attractive; but one's eye is immediately drawn to the artwork and cannot concentrate on the stamps. The stamps thus become merely an excuse for the draughtsmanship, instead of the latter being subordinated to the stamps.

Apart from such written descriptions as may be necessary, the only decoration that is really allowable is the occasional use of a neat frame-line to draw attention to a particularly important specimen; absolute simplicity is the height of refinement.

Emphasis is also obtainable by the use of little paper arrows which can be attached to the page to indicate a particularly interesting item. They can also be employed to point out the position of flaws or other variations in a stamp's design, but if they are to overlap the stamp, be sure that there is no chance of their sticking to it, or the stamp may be ruined. Do resist the temptation to mark every dot and dash with an arrow, or your pages will look like scenes from the Battle of Hastings!

Colour should be used very sparingly. Red ink is, perhaps, the least objectional, and can be used for underlining, for initials, or in places where a certain modest emphasis is required. Crude colours, such as violet or green, are sure to clash with the colours of your stamps and are to be avoided.

Let your aim be to have a collection which does not allow the beholder to miss its strong points, and yet has the good manners not to shout them blatantly at him.

As regards the extent of your descriptive writing-up, you must be guided by your intention in forming the collection. For a collection arranged according to a particular catalogue, it will probably be enough to include the name of the country, the date of issue, its watermark, perforation, etc, but so long as your writing-up does not overweight the page, there is no harm in adding details as to printers, designers, etc, very brief descriptions of the designs of the stamps (below each) may also be included where they are of interest, as such descriptions attract people who may not understand the attention you pay to purely philatelic details.

In 'thematic' collections which deal purely with the stories told by individual stamps – zoological, historical, or other similar displays – the descriptive matter must be very carefully selected as there is so much that can be said and yet the stamps must not be lost in a wilderness of words. If a large amount of text is really necessary try to balance it by including a large item, such as a cover or miniature sheet, on the page rather than just one or two stamps. If you really know your stamps you can always supplement the written descriptions verbally, and this method can be made much more attractive to those examining the collection.

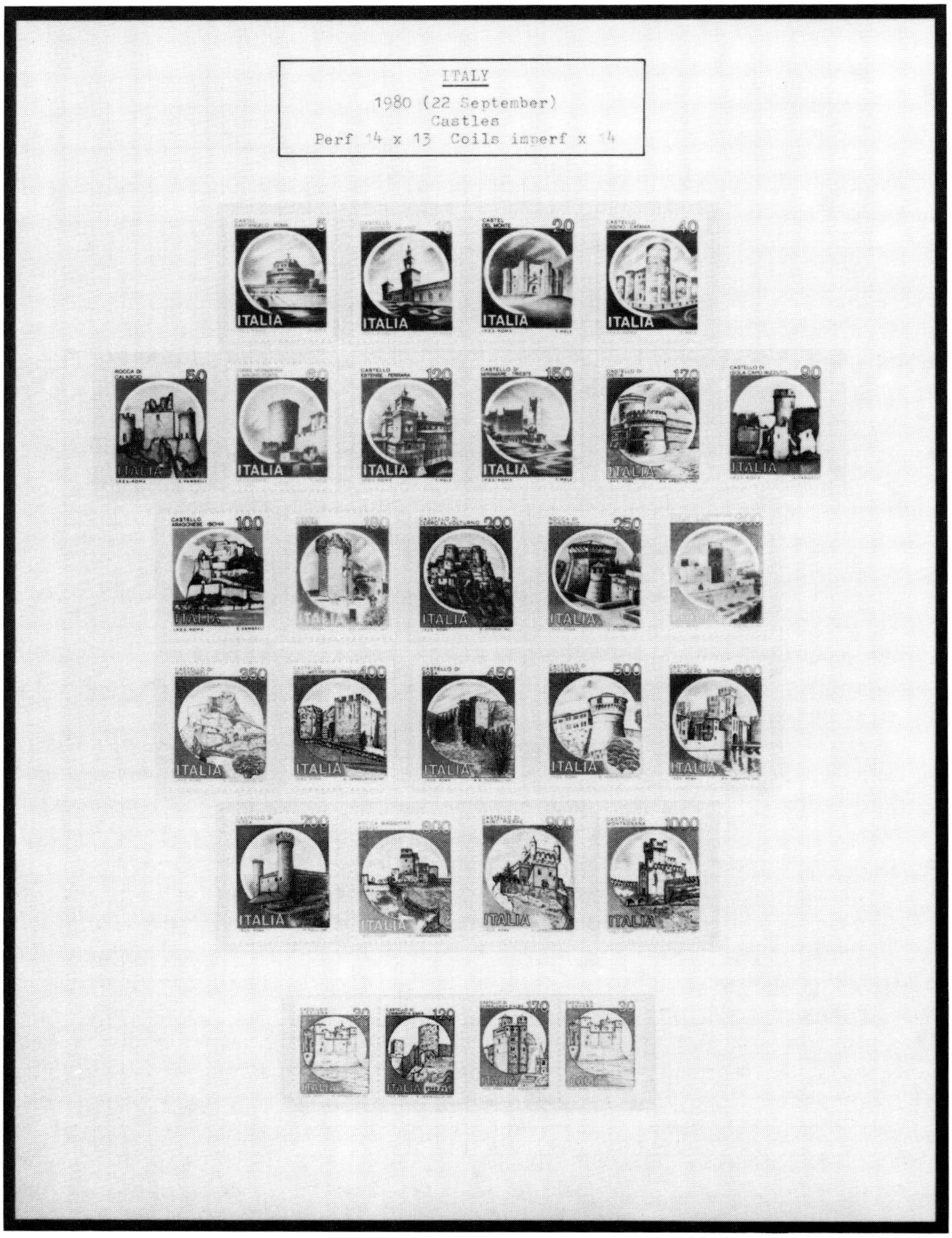

1 A neat arrangement of stamps of the same shape

Sometimes it may be advisable to write the descriptions of all the stamps together below the set, particularly where the descriptions are too long to go easily beneath the individual stamps. Such a course should be avoided wherever possible, as reference to the descriptions is more difficult where they are not close to the stamps to which they apply.

In highly specialised collections, particularly in those which are formed to show the result of a particular line of research, the owner must be allowed to explain the various stages of study by rather copious notes, but even in these collections the writing-up should be confined to the minimum necessary for that purpose. Enlarged sketches of particular details are often very helpful in reducing the amount of description required, though their production is not within the capacity of all. An enlarged photograph of a stamp or a portion of it may be used as a substitute, the important details being emphasised, if necessary, in ink. Photostats may also be useful in this respect.

Apart from such enlarged sketches, designs of an artistic character may be regarded as permissible when they serve as title-pages to an album or country, while sketch maps, either in black or colours, can also be included. These latter are particularly useful in postal history collections for indicating mail routes.

To sum up, the following general rules should be followed:

1. Do not use decoration or colour to such an extent that they are no longer subsidiary to the stamps.
2. Do not include more written description than is absolutely necessary to explain your stamps, having regard to the purpose for which the particular collection is formed.

ARRANGING A GENERAL COLLECTION

The preceding sections have been devoted to the preparation of what might be called the elements of our picture. We have selected the album, the stamps have been prepared and sorted into issues, and we have chosen the style of writing, so that we may now go ahead with the arrangement of these elements to form a display that will be artistic as well as efficient. All our efforts at good lettering would be ineffective if the stamps were poorly arranged.

As we see only one page at a time when we look at a collection each should be considered as a separate picture and built up as if it were the only one, the sole link between the individual pages being uniformity of style.

Good display is a combination of symmetry, balance, and lucidity, and is not difficult to obtain if a few principles are observed.

By symmetry is understood the grouping of the elements so that the left side is the same as the right, while balance is a grouping that is pleasing to the eye. For example, if the stamps are arranged in perfect alignment in a number of rows of equal length they will be symmetrical, but they will not be balanced because they will appear bottom-heavy on account of the downward pull on the eye.

To facilitate arrangement practically all blank leaves sold for stamp collections have the centre lines of the *quadrillé* pattern marked by a heavier stroke where they intersect or touch the outer line. The vertical line is the more important and it is on either side of it that the stamps should be arranged. In this we are favoured, since most stamps are little rectangles perfectly balanced in themselves and therefore often requiring nothing more than a symmetrical disposition on either side of the centre line. Often collectors shirk the effort of balancing their stamps by starting each issue against the left-hand margin, leaving the right side more or less blank according to the length of the set. Such arrangements are obviously unsightly because they disregard both symmetry and balance, and while they may be suitable for dealers' stock-books, they should be avoided by collectors aiming at the good appearance of their collections. To help in arranging your stamps you may find it useful to make a rule from thin card with the outer edges of the *quadrillé*, centre, quarter, three-quarters and any other useful divisions marked off along one edge. This can be run down the album page to facilitate the counting of *quadrillé* squares when arranging stamps. Such a gadget can be very handy when covers or other large items have to be centred on the page.

Some collectors prefer not to mount their stamps always in straight lines. They may, for example, bring the outer stamps of a line rather below the level of the others, other lines being adjusted to give an artistic effect to the whole page.

Provided that such an arrangement is not carried to excess, as when the stamps on a page are arranged in diamonds or circles, there is not very much to be said against it, except that it makes the inclusion of the headings and notes more difficult. For the ordinary collector, however, the straight-line method is best, where the stamps in a set are all of the same size.

2a A disjointed arrangement – the result of having the top and bottom rows as the longest

2b The same stamps – by slightly altering the rows a much better arrangement is obtained

When stamps are of varying sizes, as in many pictorial issues, a more difficult problem presents itself, and it is sometimes debated whether it is best to disregard symmetry and place the stamps in order of value or to make symmetry the first consideration. There should be no hesitation in choosing appearance in preference to numerical order. As a rule it is possible with a little thought to effect a compromise whereby balance is obtained without moving some of the values more than a little way from their correct positions.

If it is impossible to balance certain shapes in one line, for example when there are three tall stamps and one broad one in a set, it is better to place the odd one on a separate line.

Whenever the high values of a long set are in a different unit of currency, or if they differ from the low values by design or type, they should be on a line by themselves. It is in fact a general principle that some endeavour should always be made to group similar parts of a set. If there are several shades or dies of a stamp they should all be in the same line and not partly on two rows; this is not so much a question of balance as of lucidity of display.

In all questions relating to the effective arrangement of his stamps, the collector should disregard any consideration of economy of space. The small saving achieved by using less leaves will be far outweighed by the loss of attractiveness caused by overcrowding.

So far the study of arrangement has been in regard to the right and left sides of the page, but the upper and lower halves, although less important, should be given some consideration. The mistake to avoid is in having too many stamps at the top of the page, resulting in top-heaviness, or at the bottom which is equally inartistic. Owing to the optical downward pull already referred to, the line on which these two halves balance is not the horizontal half-way line, but at a point slightly above it and known as the optical centre or eye-line.

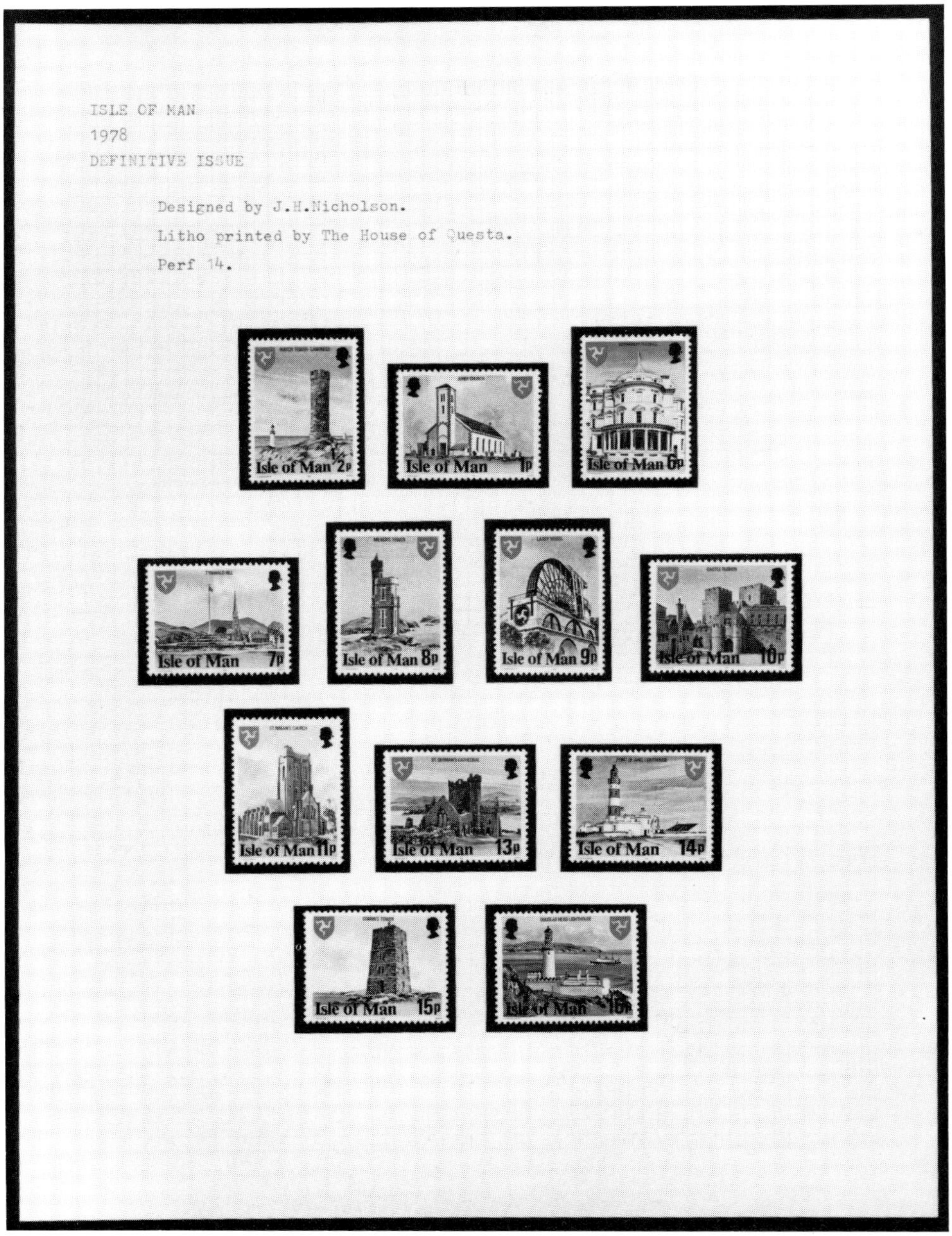

3a Stamps arranged in numerical order

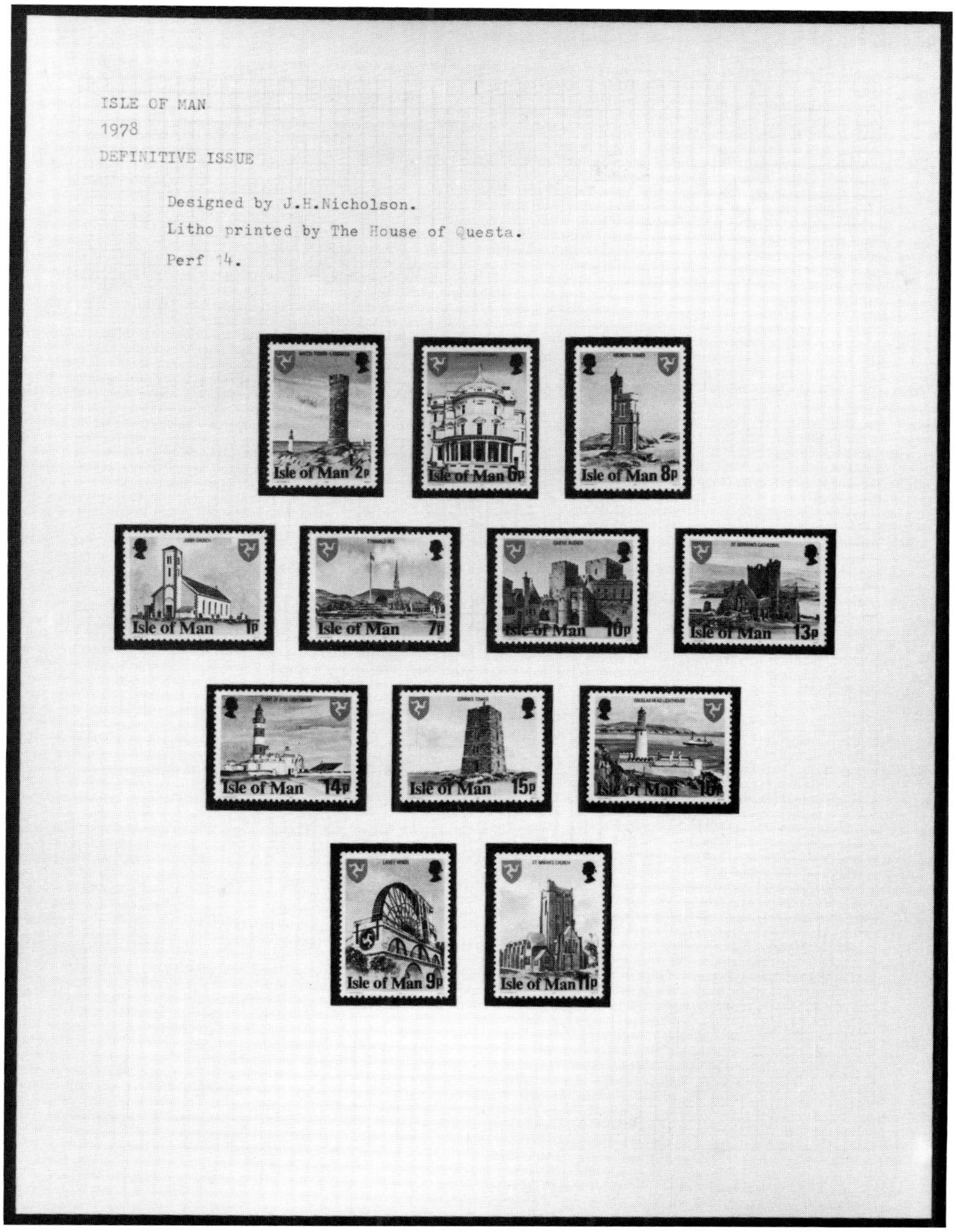

3b The same stamps arranged symmetrically – an alternative would have been to rearrange the third row shown in the previous illustration

For this reason a choice stamp will always receive quicker attention if placed a third of the way down the middle of the page. This point should be remembered when it is intended to mount a single cover or a large block on the page. If stamps are being arranged in five rows the second and third from the top should be the longest, the others shorter in varying degrees. It is surprising what variety of arrangement can be made with the other rows once the eye-line row has been established. The importance of the point can be judged from the two illustrations, the first showing the mistake of making the top and bottom rows the longest, and resulting in a disjointed display.

The spacing of the stamps has a considerable bearing on the appearance of the finished work, and the number of squares that will be left between each stamp should be determined and retained as much as possible throughout the collection. Most leaves are ruled three squares to the centimetre; in this gauge 'two squares' spacing will be found the most generally effective; 'three squares' is good between large stamps or if it is desired to give the collection a very roomy appearance; 'one square' spacing is too close and really suitable only for small leaves.

A uniform spacing between the rows should also be maintained as nearly as possible throughout the collection, although a variation is sometimes desirable if it permits the better filling of a page. The number of rows to an average page will depend on the amount of writing and the size of the stamps; five rows usually gives a pleasing effect, or six if there is only one heading.

Where the page has a heavy printed frame-border stamps should not be mounted too near it, but where the page has a central *quadrillé*-ruled area without a frame, the outer stamps can, if necessary, be placed within one square's distance from the edge of the *quadrillé* area.

When about to begin the work of arranging, the leaves should be taken out of the cover and ruled in readiness for the heading of the country. There is usually a wide margin above the *quadrillé* ground for this purpose, and a feint pencil line should be drawn about 5 mm from the top of the squares.

At this point a timely hint that will result in better work and save the loss of many expensive leaves is to arrange all the stamps, at the same time making the necessary notes in pencil before starting any of the final writing-up in ink. In this way mistakes are easily corrected, arrangements altered if necessary, and headings better centred.

If catalogue numbers are required, these should always be written in pencil, as otherwise the page will have to be scrapped if any rearrangement of its contents is undertaken, or if the catalogue is revised.

For those who feel themselves capable of centring the headings correctly above each issue it will be sufficient to make abbreviated notes in the margin when arranging, but most collectors will be well advised to pencil in the complete headings as they will appear finally. After a little experience it is possible to judge from the rough notes how much space the headings will take and thereby start at the exact spot that will ensure them beginning and ending at equal distances from the centre line. If written lightly all the pencil notes are easily rubbed out when the page is finished. When writing-up a black-leaf album, notes will have to be made on separate pieces of paper.

Assuming that the collection is a straightforward one to be arranged in the same order as the catalogue with just the most necessary details, all that need be included above each issue is the date, title or purpose of the issue, watermark and perforation.

If the name of the country is placed as already suggested in the top margin, the date of issue should not come nearer than the second line of the *quadrillé*; this will leave the equivalent of three squares while the remaining sub-headings may have two squares between them and again two squares between the last and the top of the stamps. Leave three or four squares between the rows.

If there is more than one issue on a page, at least three or four lines should be left between one issue and the next heading, but this should be increased if necessary to avoid leaving a big gap at the foot of the page. It is strongly recommended that the stamps are placed loosely in their approximate positions on the page and moved about until the best effect is obtained before any mounting is done.

Always look a few issues ahead to avoid arranging three-quarters of a page only to find that you will not get the whole of the next set in the space left. It is nearly always preferable to expand when this occurs, rather than to split an issue.

When arranging varieties, judgement should be used to determine whether comparison with the normal stamp would be useful or not. A stamp of a different die, for example, should be placed alongside the normal in the set with 'I' and 'II' written above them, but errors such as inverted surcharges, wrong spellings, etc, will attract greater attention if placed with appropriate description below the normal issue.

If used stamps are included in the collection as an alternative to unused, they will, of course, take their places in their respective sets, but where unused and used stamps are both collected, they should be mounted as distinct sets and not mixed together. If the series is of moderate length it will be possible to get unused and used sets on the same page, but with longer issues a separate page will be required for each. As already stated, it is advisable to avoid splitting sets, but in this instance unused and used can be regarded as separate sets.

The normal unused and used sets should precede the pages allotted to errors and varieties of the same, except where these have to be near the normals for comparison, or where you only have one or two varieties which will fit into available space at the foot of your normal pages.

The question of leaving blank spaces for stamps you have not yet got must depend on your decision as to the scope of your collection. You may aim to get everything listed in the catalogue, or you can whittle down the lists by excluding shades or perforations or minor varieties. You may feel sure that you will never pay more than a certain sum for a stamp, and this will give you another line of delimitation. It is therefore advisable, in planning the main pages of your album, to allow space only for those stamps you intend or hope to get, and to camouflage judiciously the absence of those which you know will never grace your collection. Errors and varieties can always find space on extra pages, but a gap in the normal issue which can never be filled is a reminder of incompleteness.

When a volume has thus been arranged and the headings prepared the writing-up in ink may be started. The names of countries should be done first, as if they are in larger lettering than the other headings they will require a larger pen. A little fancy work may also be permitted such as a red initial or the whole name in red underlined with black, which is very effective. Whatever colour or style the headings are written in, care should be taken that they are well centred as it is the spot the eye will see first. This is easily done by writing the name out on a spare piece of *quadrillé* paper, counting the number of squares it takes, and marking the length on the actual page. For the other headings above the issues, guidance for length will have to be obtained from the pencilled notes.

If any underlining is to be done it should be left till the last and carried out with a ruling or draughtsman's pen, to which reference has already been made in Part Three. With either of these pens a very fine and regular line can be drawn without fear of the ink running along the rule.

When all the lettering has been finished and the ink thoroughly dry the pencil marks can be erased from the page. It then remains to mount the stamps in position and replace the leaves in the binder.

ARRANGING THEMATIC COLLECTIONS

When the collector is dealing with a thematic collection – for example, a zoological collection – a much more interesting task is presented; the question of the order in which the stamps were issued does not occur (the collection may, in fact, contain stamps from many different countries), but merely how best to arrange them in order to illustrate the subject.

Balance and symmetry can, of course, still be observed and some ingenuity will be needed to reconcile these factors with the need for telling one's stamp story in the proper sequence, or at least approximately so. In the 'zoo' collection, for example, animals should not be mixed with reptiles or birds unless the story requires it, and it may be preferable to keep the different groups of mammals together.

Again, if the life of Columbus is the subject of a collection, stamps depicting early events, or bearing portraits of him when a young man, should precede those which deal with his later life. Here and there, it will be necessary to allow oneself a little licence but, generally speaking, the necessary grouping can be achieved without disregarding balance or symmetry. A good knowledge of stamp designs, gained from the stamp catalogue, will be helpful, for it may then be possible to select an alternative stamp showing the same person, place or event, instead of one which will not fit your arrangement.

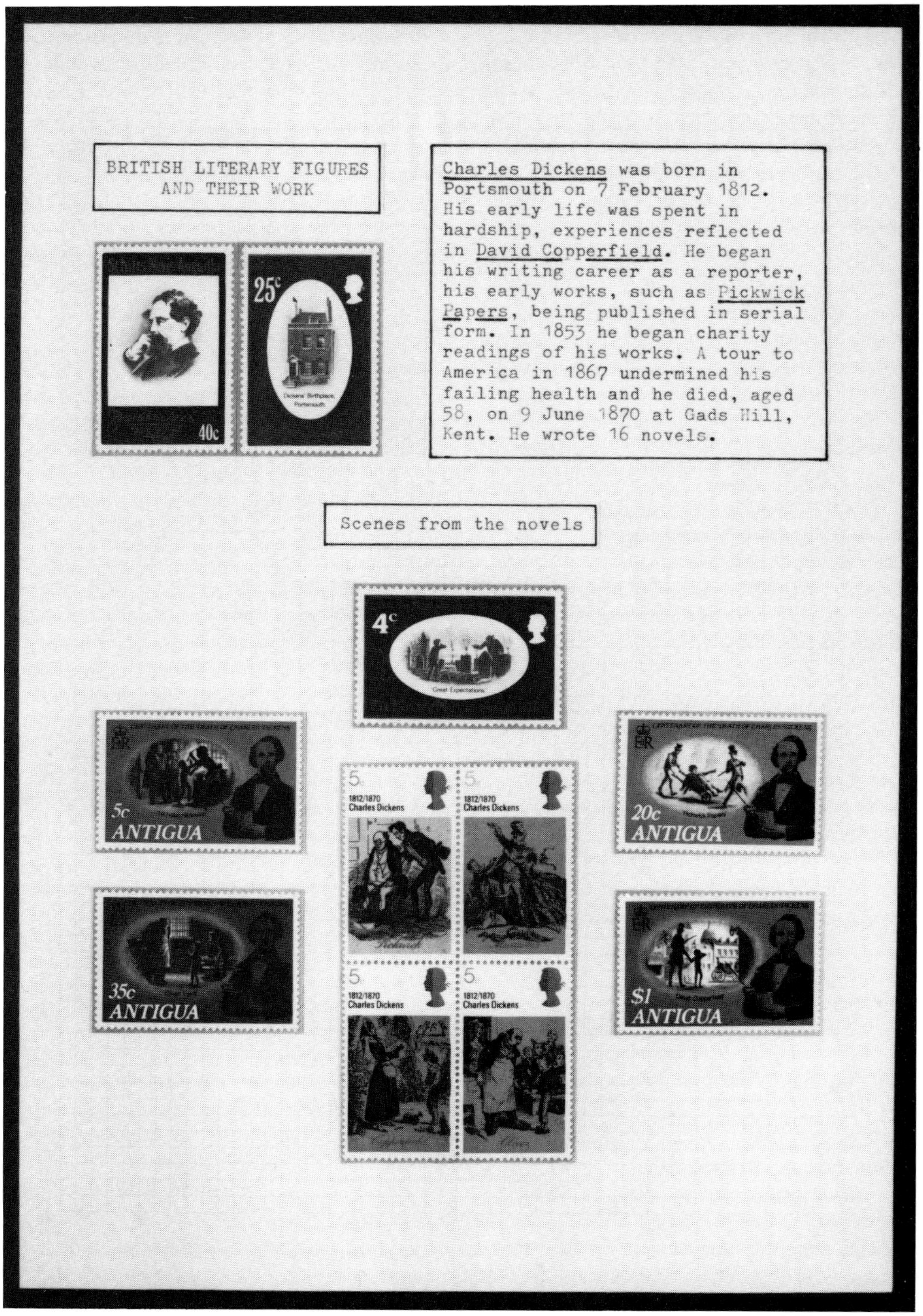

4 A page from a thematic collection written-up with labels. The stamps have been mounted on pale grey paper

It is not always possible, however, to select an appropriately shaped stamp to fit the story you are telling. Often a page from a thematic collection will contain stamps each of which is a different shape and size. When this occurs strict symmetry will have to be abandoned; this does not mean however, that balance should be abandoned as well.

Such pages will require greater thought in layout, and skilful use of descriptive matter to provide balance with the stamps. It is possible that some thematic collections will require almost every page to be treated in this way, and each page is likely to be quite different in its arrangement of stamps and text. Some collectors may even prefer this style of arrangement to the strict symmetrical one. Such pages should, of course, be arranged so that the story being told appears in a logical and easy to follow manner. The individual pages should also appear to be part of a whole. To some extent this will be achieved through the use of a uniform style of lettering. It can be enhanced by such small points as the positioning of titles and captions and, perhaps, by mounting the material to be displayed on a neutral coloured background.

In thematic collections, the values of the stamps are disregarded and only one stamp of each design or subject is usually needed. It should, of course, be selected with careful reference to the general colour balance of the page you are arranging, if there is sufficient scope for choice, for some colours kill those of the adjacent stamps, and while this cannot be avoided when complete sets have to be arranged in a general collection, you have more freedom of choice in a collection in which the stamp designs are the important factor.

ARRANGING SPECIALISED COLLECTIONS

The arrangement of a specialised collection to show the result of the owner's studies and researches presents many difficulties. In some such collections there is much to say about every stamp, while in others several pages of written introduction seem necessary before the stamps themselves are reached. Remembering the rules already laid down, the owners of specialised collections should study the art of expressing themselves concisely. If the collection is one which will be displayed at meetings and exhibitions, the descriptions must be very lucid, and a statement divided up into short paragraphic notes, logically arranged, is very much more effective than descriptive notes written in the style of an article. Every word that is not absolutely necessary should be left out.

Often a great deal of verbal description can be avoided by the use of small sketches, illustrating on a large scale details not readily apparent from an examination of the stamp. Even a rough sketch, by a collector who lays no claim to artistic skill, will be well worth the doing. Space will sometimes be saved by making a large-scale sketch or outline of a stamp and indicating on it all varieties shown in the collection.

To draw attention to varieties on stamps in the middle of large blocks, a strip of transparent paper may be run across the block and on this an explanatory sketch may be drawn indicating both the position of the variety in the block and the details to which it is desired to draw attention. If a sketch is not necessary, an indicator arrow may be affixed to the transparent paper.

Those who have no courage for sketching can make use of enlarged photographs of the stamp sections to which they want to draw particular attention. It is not advisable to entrust such work to a photographer inexperienced in stamp work, for the non-philatelic world has strange ideas as to what may be done in order to fix stamps up for photographing.

The question of balance and symmetry takes on quite a different aspect from that presented in a general collection. A general collection will contain rows of stamps and, usually, lines of writing, but in a specialised collection there is often a disproportionate amount of writing, to which may be added sketches, photographs, tables of settings, etc, while the stamps themselves may be supplemented by covers, and there will often be blocks, pairs, and even sheets to deal with. Obviously the proper arrangement of such a mass of material and information is a complex problem, but one very fascinating to solve.

If the collection is one of those in which specialised study has been superimposed on a backbone consisting of a straightforward display, the simplified collection might well be arranged first, as if it were part of a general collection, i.e. the straightforward issues, unused and used, will be allotted to their pages and arranged and written-up as already described.

If blocks and pairs run right through the collection in addition to singles, the collector will have to decide whether he will put these larger items on separate pages, or group them with the singles. Pages bearing nothing but blocks of four tend to look too heavy, and in many collections an effective grouping can be obtained by putting the blocks and pairs with the single specimens. Some collectors with plenty of money go so far as to take as many stamps as are necessary to secure effective balance, even where some of them are duplicates, but with a little ingenuity the less lavish collector will be able to group non-specialised material, blocks, pairs, and singles, effectively in a homogeneous and straightforward collection which, when arranged and written-up, will form the backbone for a specialised study.

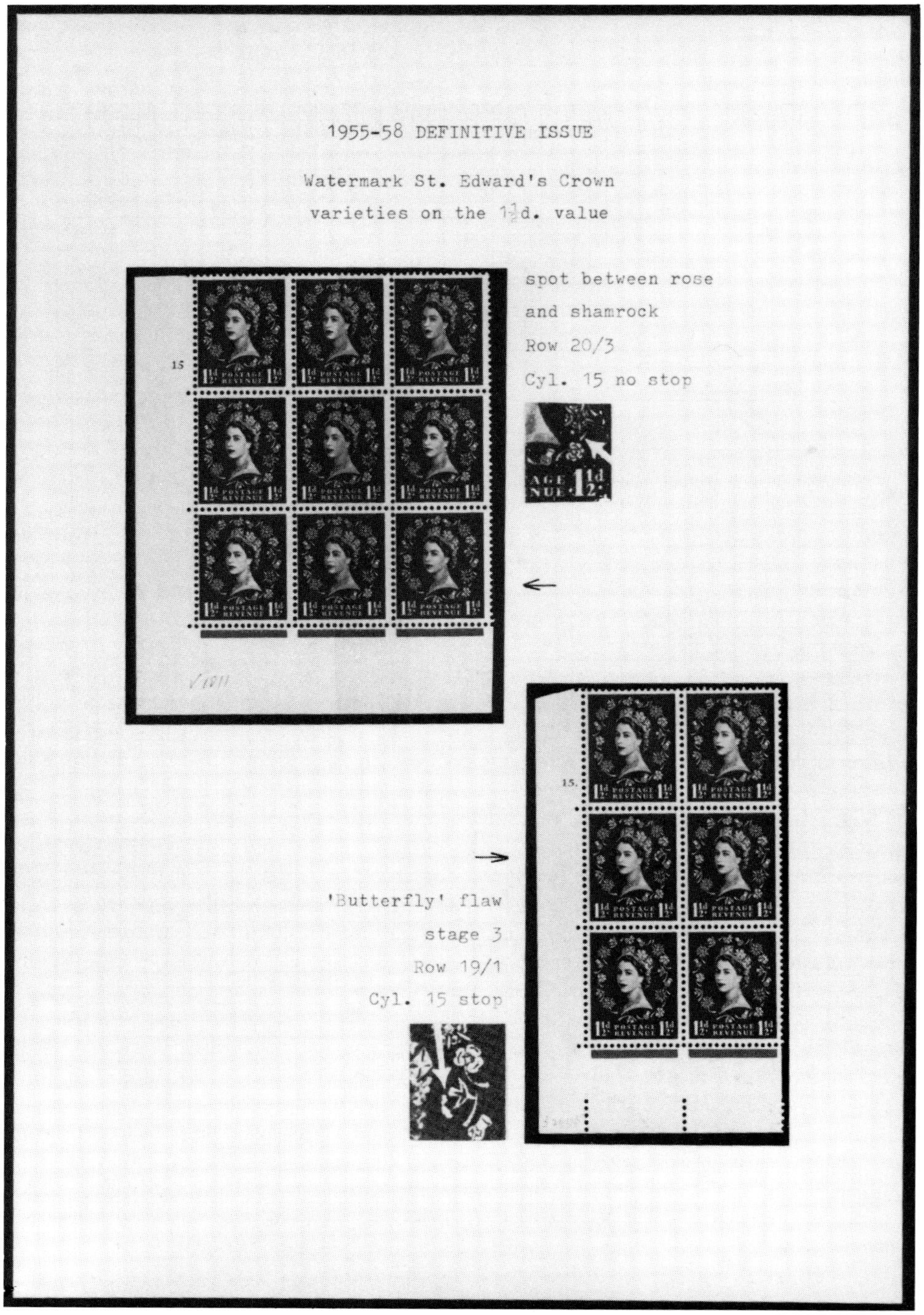

5 A page from a specialised collection. Englarged photographs show details of the variety, arrows point out the affected stamp

6 A photograph used to illustrate a number of varieties on the same stamp. This avoids the scrappy effect of several sketches on a page. The reference numbers are repeated above or below the corresponding stamps

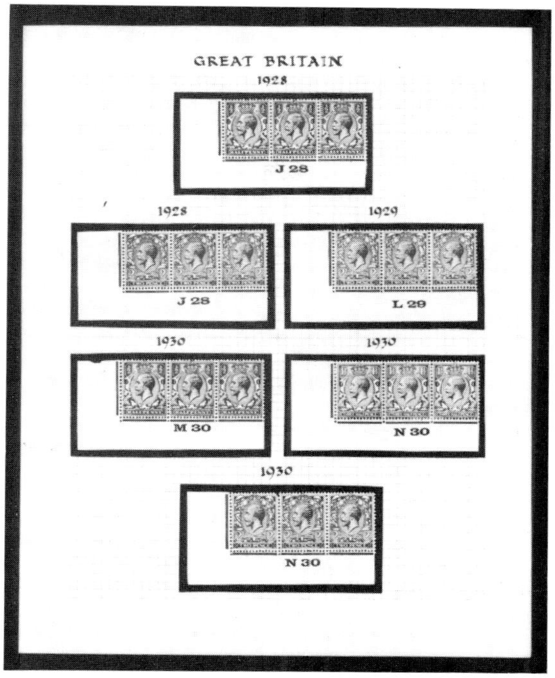

7 Controls and other pieces with a lop-sided appearance may be improved by mounting on black paper

Next group the special items of each issue (or value, if the collection is on a large scale), and divide these into sections according to the class of variety they show. Thus re-entries, postmarks, shades, covers, and so on, will form separate classes, each of which can be arranged on its page or pages, though division between the straightforward part of the collection and the specialised should not be too rigid. For example, an odd cover, not specially needed anywhere else, will often serve to round off a page only partly filled with a particular issue.

There will also be many occasions when a particular specimen is needed to illustrate points in two sections of the collection; for example, a stamp which shows a marked retouch and which also bears an outstanding type of postmark. When this occurs the stamp should be placed in the section in which it will be most useful for comparison, and a written cross-reference will have to be made in its alternative position, the album pages being numbered (in pencil) in order that this may be done.

Stamps with marginal paper attached present a subsidiary problem. Marginal paper that gives no information (i.e. which does not bear an imprint, control, plate number, or other indication which teaches something of the history of the particular stamp), adds nothing to a collection *per se*, but can help determine sheet positions, etc and is probably best not removed. For better-priced items, marginal or corner copies often command a premium, and this is another reason why tearing or cutting off margins may be unwise.

If one or two stamps in a set have marginal plate numbers attached, it may be possible to preserve symmetry by doing some slight violence to numerical order. It would be better, however, to complete the main set with non-marginal stamps and allot a separate line to your plate numbers below.

A corner block with margins on two sides, or a strip of three stamps with two margins, the bottom one showing a 'control', are awkward things to arrange neatly on an album page, for from their very nature they are lop-sided.

The best solution to arranging such pieces (and this applies to a collection of such items also) is to mount each separate block or strip on a piece of thin black paper, or in a protective mount, a small margin of which is allowed to project all round. The black mount is then treated as the unit and placed on the album page as balance and symmetry require. The eye sees block and mount as a whole and the effect of lop-sidedness disappears.

If a collection is arranged on these lines, we shall have, in each issue, first a straightforward display of the normal stamps in singles, with pairs and blocks in addition, if these are taken, used stamps being grouped after the unused, either on the same page when space permits, or on following pages. Then will come pages devoted to errors (where these will not find a convenient niche on the general pages), varieties, postmarks, and so on, all grouped in logical sequence – a sequence, by the way, that reminds us that essays, proofs, artists' sketches and 'specimen' stamps should precede each issue, where they are available.

In arranging these specialised pages, the balance to be aimed at is rather the balance of the advertisement, than the mathematical regularity suggested for a general collection. Symmetry, too, as with thematic collections, will have a different meaning, for it will not always be possible to group illustrations, descriptive notes, photographs and sketches so that they fall evenly on either side of the centre line of the page. The collection may contain, for example, a page on which there is a block of nine stamps, a fifty word note and a table of the setting. Such a page may look best with a diagonal arrangement of the block and the table, with the notes arranged to conform.

Every page of a specialised collection will present its own problem, and half the pleasure in arranging a collection to look its best consists in solving these problems to one's own satisfaction.

ARRANGING COVERS

The collecting of illustrated first day of issue and other commemorative covers is a very popular aspect of stamp collecting. As the entire front of the envelope is of importance in this type of collecting 'arrangement' is virtually non-existent, the covers are simply mounted symmetrically on the album page with photograph corners and any necessary descriptive matter added above or below the item. However, the weight of the covers, and their bulk, makes this method unsuitable when a large collection of covers has to be arranged. A much better solution is to house the covers in one of the many specially produced cover albums available and described in Part One of this book. The covers may be slipped straight into the transparent pockets or mounted on the thin card inserts usually supplied with such albums. Two covers can be held back to back in each pocket.

Such albums have one drawback however, usually no provision is made for writing-up, the inserts allowing no more than a narrow border around the cover. Often, of course, illustrated covers require no writing-up, all that needs to be said is contained on the cover front in the form of illustration, stamps, postmark and, possibly, cachet.

If additional descriptive matter is required, two solutions present themselves: the writing-up can be placed in the pocket below (if the leaf holds two covers) or the back of the pocket on the preceding page (if a single cover leaf); or an interleaf can be used.

The first method has one major drawback in that the number of covers the album is able to hold is halved. The second method is a much better answer to the problem but will probably require that the interleaves are made to measure. A stiff good quality cartridge paper should be used, cut to the same size as the transparent leaves, and punched to fit the binder. Both sides of the paper can be used for writing-up and the full capacity of the album is preserved. Such interleaves may also be used to provide a title page for the album.

Many covers contain informative insert cards, these can be mounted with photograph corners on the interleaving sheet as an alternative to writing-up.

ARRANGING A POSTAL HISTORY COLLECTION

The strict definition of the term 'postal history' implies a much wider field of research into all aspects of the posts, many of which are not capable of expression through a 'philatelic' collection, than is covered by most collectors when they use it. The term is often, if incorrectly, applied to the study and collecting of 'pre-stamp' material; postal markings, postal routes, rates and services, and similar facets of philately also fall within this field. Much of the material in a postal history collection will consist of covers and similar pieces.

It would seem that such a collection presents the same problems as the collecting of illustrated covers described above. However, unlike a collection of illustrated covers, it will almost certainly require writing-up, often to a considerable extent. Often, too, both sides

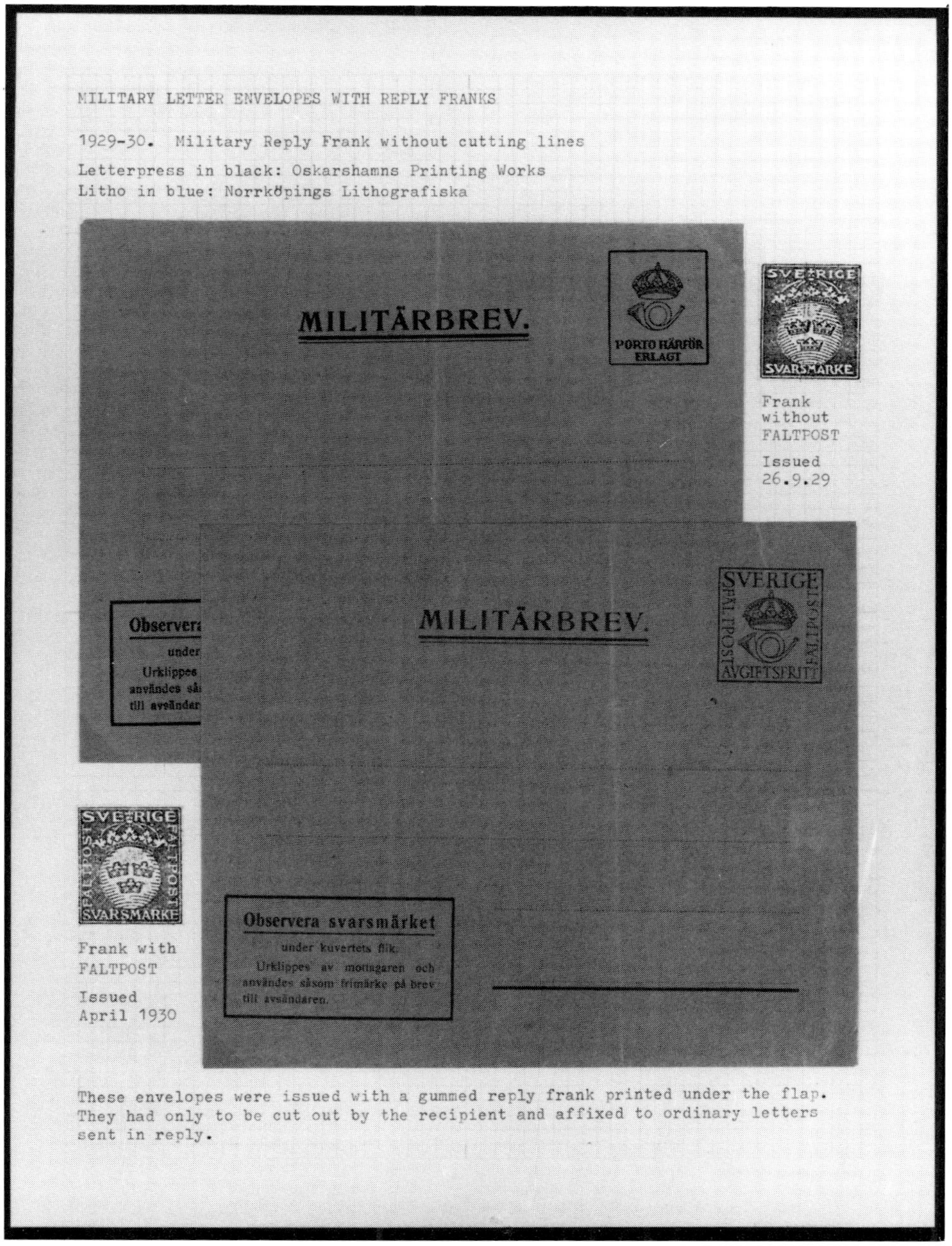

8 Covers with reverse markings. Here a photostat has been used alongside the appropriate cover

of an item will be of importance, a backstamp on the reverse of a cover may be a vital part of a postal route study, for example. The answer to such a problem would, at first glance, be to use a cover album with transparent pockets. Both sides of the cover can then be easily and safely examined, and writing-up can be accommodated on an interleaf as already described. However, there is a disadvantage in this solution. The exhibit, like Gaul, will have been divided into three parts – one leaf of description, another showing the front of the item, and a third, completely isolated from the description, showing the item's reverse. Separation of description and cover may be acceptable with illustrated covers, where most of the information is readily relayed by the cover itself; it should be avoided, if possible, in a collection where item and description are closely related.

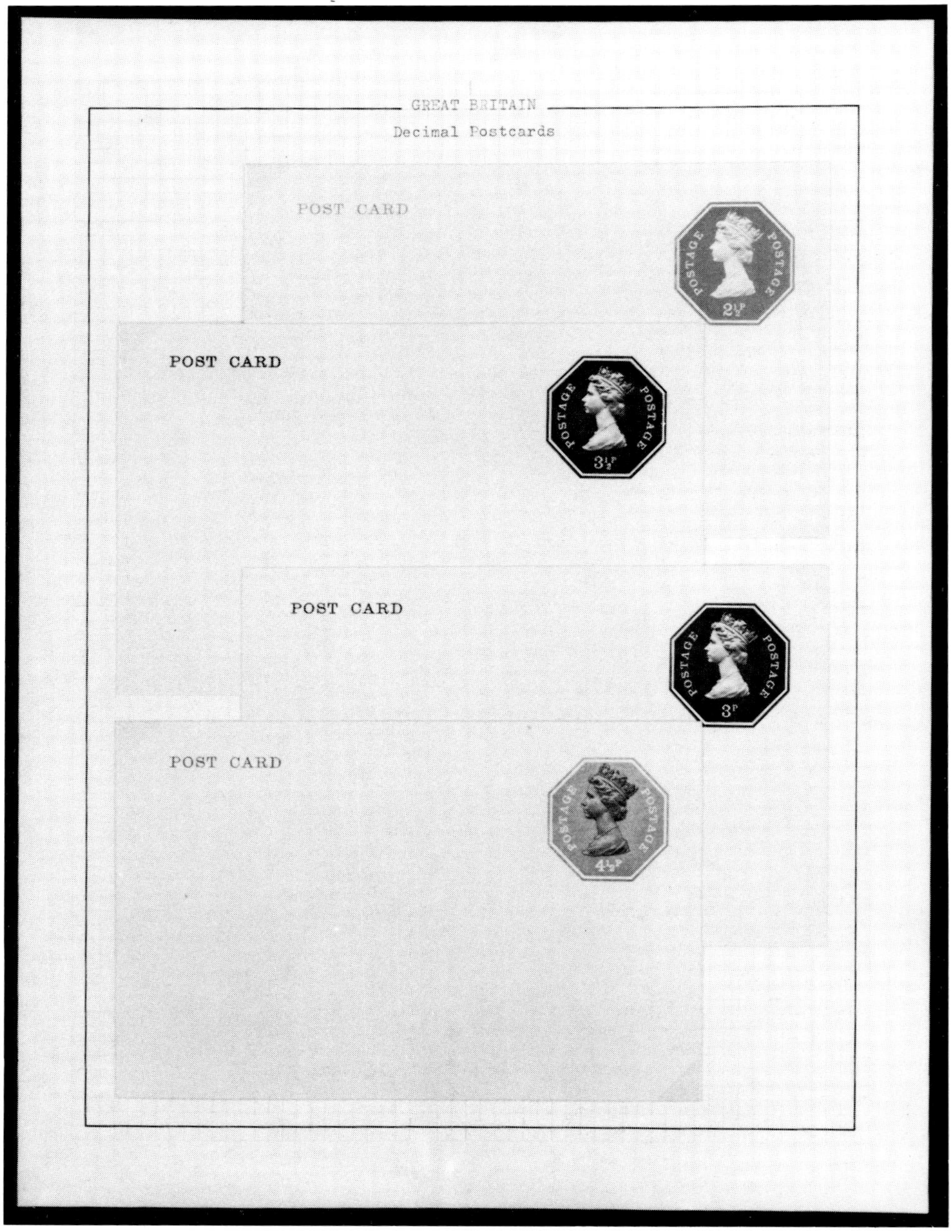

9 There is little of importance on these cards other than the stamps. Overlapping has allowed four to be mounted on a page

The most widely accepted method of overcoming this problem is to mount the cover on a standard album leaf, with description, and to include drawings of any relevant markings that appear on the reverse. If you feel unsure of your ability to draw, photostats or photographs may be the answer.

If tracings of the marks are made use a finely pointed pencil and be very careful not to press too hard, if you do you are likely to mark your, possible valuable, piece. To avoid any danger of spillage do not use ink anywhere near your collection. Pencil drawings may be inked in later. It may be helpful, when attempting a drawing or tracing, to turn the mark you wish to copy upside down. The unfamiliar direction of the letters makes them easier to follow accurately. The drawings are best done on a separate piece of paper (avoiding the possibility of spoiling an album page) and mounted in place with a stamp hinge or a dab of gum. The drawings may, of course, be finished in colour if that is how they appear on the item concerned.

Occasionally a piece may be opened out to show any backstamps. Sometimes, too, the contents of a letter are important to the study being undertaken. If the item is a folded letter it should be displayed front outwards (unless the letter is the only important part) and the relevant section included as part of the writing-up. You may also wish to include a photographic copy of the letter, or the letter may be loose, this can be mounted on a separate page.

Many early letters are very thick. Large photograph corners will be required to mount them. The number of pages that may be safely contained in a binder will, of course, be restricted, and spacers will probably be required to prevent the leaves from fanning out. Some attempt should be made to avoid mounting covers in the same position on each page, this will help reduce the pressure on them when the album is closed. This hazard is particularly likely to occur when there are several pages containing a single cover.

No mention has been made of overlapping covers. In general this is best avoided. With most items it will probably not be possible anyhow, either because of their thickness or the importance of their postal markings. Occasionally, however, on a page showing, for example, covers with different printed 'post paid' impressions, where these are the only things of significance, overlapping may not only save space but make a philatelic point more easily by grouping the relevant items together.

Postal history collections will often benefit from maps. These should be drawn to show the relevant points, such as stages on a mail route, rather than taken from an atlas or similar source which contains too much confusing detail. An atlas can, of course, provide the basis for your drawing. Many other non-philatelic items may appear to fit nicely into your chosen subject, but it should be remembered that a postal history collection's prime stress should be on its philatelic content, it should not be swamped with maps, pictures, and so on. Include such things only if they have an important part to play in your study.

PROTECTING LARGE ITEMS

Many collections contain items, such as large envelopes, sheets of stamps, etc, that will not fit onto an ordinary album page. How to protect them from damage and have them readily available for examination is often a problem

The best answer is to make your own storage system. Large sheets of stiff cartridge paper or thin card can be cut to a suitable size to take the largest item and any writing-up. Holes should be punched in one side of the cut sheets, they can then be stored between two slightly larger pieces of thick card punched with matching holes through which tapes can hold the whole collection together. Those with the necessary ability may, of course, make a more eleaborate binder. An alternative method is to store the sheets in a suitable box.

You may wish to protect the sheets with a transparent covering, particularly advisable if the item is flimsy. If this is decided a suitable material must be used. ICI 'Melinex' is probably best for this purpose as it is believed to contain no dangerous chemicals that could harm stamps. However it is not usually available in the small quantities required by most collectors. Cellophane is not recommended as a covering material unless a substantial backing board is used. It quickly shrinks and unless attached to a firm backing the sheet it covers will buckle and the items mounted on it may be damaged. Plastic folders are obtainable from stationers, these may contain chemicals that will eventually harm your stamps and should not be used for long term storage of philatelic items unless they are protected by a suitable interleaf.

10 A large and flimsy item in a protective sleeve

The best method of using the 'Melinex' (if obtainable) is to make a pocket from two sheets of it, joining them together along three sides with double-sided adhesive tape. The written-up page may be slid between them and your stamps or covers will be fully protected, kept away from the adhesive tape and be easily removable. Two sheets can be stored in the same protector back to back. Do not seal the item completely as this will cut off air and prevent it from breathing.

DISPLAYS

Whatever the collector's opinion as to the desirability of properly arranging and writing-up a collection, there are occasions when it is absolutely necessary for the collector to deal with at least a portion of it. At a display to a philatelic society it is a matter of courtesy to those who will be present, while any attempt to gain a cup or medal at a stamp exhibition is unlikely to be successful if no attention has been paid to arrangement.

Assuming that the preceding sections of this book have been studied, the reader should be familiar with the processes necessary for making the best of a collection, but there are special considerations in connection with displays and exhibitions which call for careful thought.

In displaying stamps to members of a philatelic society regard must be paid to the method of display. At many meetings, each sheet to be shown is handed to the chairman as the owner begins to describe it, and from the chairman it passes to the other members present in rotation.

The result of this system is that only the chairman sees the stamps at the moment when the owner is talking about them, and the remaining persons present are faced with the choice between looking at the stamps when they reach them and disregarding the speaker's remarks, or of listening to the talk and missing the opportunity of examining the stamps. This method of conducting displays can only be regarded as a thoroughly bad one.

Another method, which is a great improvement, is to have the sheets of stamps laid out on a table or shown in frames during the early part of the meeting so that those present can make themselves generally familiar with the display. The talk is then given by the owner, who can be listened to without the distraction caused by stamps being passed round, and after that the audience goes back to the display to study more closely any particular items which have aroused their special interest.

At some society meetings a combination of the above methods is adopted, the pages of the collection specially referred to being handed round during the owner's talk, and the remaining pages being displayed in the room for examination before and after the main proceedings.

It is obvious that, before arranging a display, the collector must know which of these systems will be followed. If all the sheets are to be handed round during the talk the collector will have to remember that the majority of the audience will not see a particular item while it is being referred to, therefore explanations cannot be relied on to take the place of written notes on the album pages. The display must be fully written-up and deal with the essential points of the talk also, it must be realised that very few will hear what is said once the pages begin to circulate. (This prompts the suggestion that the preliminary remarks which precede the handing round of the display should contain as much of interest as possible.)

Where the stamps are exhibited separately and not handed round during the talk, the technical and other details which depend upon an examination of the stamps should be included in the write-up of the pages and the spoken comments, while not omitting reference to such details where necessary, can be extended to a more general survey of the subject.

While on this subject, perhaps a word on the selection of material for display may not be out of place. In some societies the number of pages to be shown is limited, and this, of course, necessitates careful choice where the owner has a large collection. Where there is no limiting rule it is still advisable to cut down the number of pages, and devote proper consideration to each, rather than to attempt to display hurriedly the whole of a large collection. Where the whole or part of the collection is to be displayed and not handed round, limitation need not be so drastic, but even so it is better to show too little rather than too much.

In choosing the pages for a display the best method is to try and build up a show which will convey the full interest of the subject under discussion, even if this necessitates forming a special condensed collection for the occasion instead of merely showing a selection of existing pages as they stand.

Remember that you have a particular interest in your subject, but that the majority of your audience, being either specialists in other countries or themes or else general collectors, cannot be expected to share that interest unless you are able to convey it to them in your talk and by your written notes. The stamps you show must therefore, so far as possible, have a wide appeal. Some of your audience will be able to appreciate the interest of technical points, but for others you must provide interesting sidelights on postal history, chatty descriptions of how you acquired some of your best items, remarks about the designs of the stamps, and an indication of the value of your rarities. If all collectors remembered the need for bringing out the 'general interest' of their subject when giving displays, society meetings would not be the boresome occasions they so frequently are.

It is obvious from what has been said, that the wiriting-up of the pages shown must also emphasise the interest of the display from as many angles as possible, and this is another reason for building up a special summarised collection rather than showing selected sheets, as already arranged.

EXHIBITIONS

When exhibitions, and particularly big international competitive exhibitions, are considered, different factors have to be taken into account.

You will be permitted to apply for as much space as the exhibition rules allow to a single competitor, but often you cannot be sure of getting even the space officially allotted to you, as drastic cuts are frequently made at the last minute due to pressure on space. It is best, therefore, to consider your collection in three ways: as a whole; as to the proportion required to fill the space you hope to have allotted to you in the public frames; as to what you will want to show to the public in the minimum space the committee can possibly be cruel enough to cut you down to.

Study the exhibition rules very carefully as soon as they appear, for alterations are often made. You may find that pages of a particular size are specified for display in the frames, which may involve remounting that part of your collection which is to be publicly shown. The rules may contain other restrictions, these must be strictly observed.

Looking at the collection as a whole, you are aiming to satisfy the judges that it is the best in its particular class. To do this, your notes, while as brief as possible, must convey clearly everything that is likely to influence the judges and particularly the lines of any original research you have carried out. As judges have to work hurriedly at great pressure, photographs and drawings, the meaning of which can be grasped at a glance, will be valuable aids to success.

For your display in the frames, it will be a great help if you can ascertain as early as possible what is the absolute minimum of space that is likely to be allotted to you. Collectors who have previously exhibited at international shows may be able to assist you in arriving at an estimate.

Having established a minimum space, work out a really interesting display to occupy it, introducing as much variety as possible, for most visitors to an exhibition are in the same position as many members of the audience at a philatelic society meeting – they have no special knowledge of your subject, though they are willing to be interested. To this minimum display add as many pages as may be necessary (still selected for their general interest) to fill the maximum space you hope to get. When sending your entry it is quite easy to specify that such and such pages must be shown in the frames, after which the remaining space available can be filled from pages so-and-so to so-and-so.

A point to remember when mounting stamps for exhibition is that the leaves may be subject to accidental mishandling. Stamps and other items should, therefore, be securely attached to the pages. Protective mounts that are sealed on one edge are particularly prone to stamp movement, the double sealed type, or stamp hinges, are much safer.

It is probably best that the whole of the pages which the public is likely to see, should be written-up from the 'interest' point of view, as was suggested for society displays, giving points which may not interest the judges but will attract the general collector and the man who does not collect.

Collectors may be discouraged from exhibiting at the big shows by the knowledge that some of the collections with which they will be competing have been arranged, written-up, and illustrated by professionals, who are past masters in the art of making stamps look their best. Too much importance should not, however, be attached to this. A large number of the entries, even at the great international exhibitions, are not well arranged and annotated, yet many of them get prizes, for 'writing-up' receives only a portion of the total marks allowed. The collector who is able to show a close study of the stamps, and who can present them in a neat and logical arrangement and with the necessary minimum of notes legibly written or printed, is not likely to be beaten by a competitor who relies on pretty arrangement alone.

Another type of exhibition which is becoming popular, consists of a display by members of a philatelic society in frames hung in a prominent place in the local library or institute. While pages from existing collections may be lent for this purpose, it is sometimes advisable to strike a new note, such as is afforded by mounting the stamps on black card with the descriptive notes in white ink.

Collectors who give philatelic displays to schools and clubs will find that remounting due to soiled leaves is avoided by using black card. Ready-made transparent covers known as exhibition protectors also provide an excellent means of protecting album pages from rough handling. These consist of two sheets of clear material sealed on two or three sides between which the album sheet is inserted.

Conclusion

This book is not an attempt to set down a series of hard-and-fast rules to follow when arranging a collection. There are many occasions when the collector can achieve equally good and logical results with alternative methods of arrangement, and it is purely a matter of taste which to adopt.

These notes have attempted to show some general principles, which may prove of assistance, but even to these there must be many exceptions. It is in deciding when such exceptions are justified, and in overcoming difficulties when arranging thematic and specialised collections, that the collector will find scope for ingenuity and for the expression of personality.

One word in conclusion. Many are convinced that they have no artistic flair. This is a great fallacy. Almost anyone can, with a little patience and practice, teach themselves to write or print neatly, though naturally the best work of this kind will not be done at the same rate as one s ordinary writing. Even sketches can, after a few attempts, be executed to a passable standard.

If the arrangement and writing-up of a collection is undertaken with the will to succeed, and in the conviction that time devoted to it will be time well spent, the pleasure derived from one's stamps will be greatly increased and the pride of ownership in a well-arranged and annotated collection will more than repay the time and trouble involved.

Index